Essentials of Classroom Management and Discipline

ESSENTIALS OF CLASSROOM MANAGEMENT AND DISCIPLINE

THEONA McQUEEN
University of Miami

HarperCollins*Publishers*

Executive Editor: Christopher Jennison
Project Coordination, Cover Design, and Cover Illustration:
  York Production Services
Production Manager: Michael Weinstein
Compositor: York Production Services
Printer and Binder: R. R. Donnelley & Sons Company
Cover Printer: The Lehigh Press, Inc.

Essentials of Classroom Management and Discipline

Library of Congress Cataloging-in-Publication Data

McQueen, T. (Theona)
    Essentials of classroom management and discipline, K–12 /
T. McQueen.
        p.   cm.
    Includes bibliographical references.
    ISBN 0-673-46354-0
    1. Classroom management. 2. School children—Discipline.
I. Title.
LB3013.M388   1992
371.1′024--dc20   91-24338
                                                                           CIP

91 92 93 94 9 8 7 6 5 4 3 2 1

To my Mother, Elsie Long McQueen,
who wanted to see this book completed.

Contents

List of Forms

Preface

A teacher is the object of respect and demands that require special knowledge, skills, and resources. As a preservice or beginning teacher, you are confident that you have acquired knowledge of the subject matter necessary to teach students and feel you can plan and execute a dynamic lesson, but you may not feel as confident about managing classroom behavior. You may ask yourself, "When the bell rings and the door closes and at least 30 pairs of eyes focus on me, what will I do? What will I say?" Don't panic! Just as you have learned your subject matter and how to plan and execute dynamic lessons, you can also learn how to manage your classroom effectively. This book will help develop the skills a professional teacher needs to manage classrooms and teach discipline.

There are many simplistic myths concerning teachers and their ability to manage classrooms and provide discipline. You know or probably have heard some of them. For example, you may believe that the teacher who exerts good discipline does not smile before Christmas, or you may believe that "teachers are born" and instinctively know how to teach and manage classrooms. Historically, researchers have focused on a broad spectrum of possible qualities and characteristcs of effective classroom managers, such as stature, age, personality, and even race. Other studies have attempted to determine whether the quality and amount of teacher preparation affects teachers' ability to teach and manage classrooms. Current research efforts are being directed at analyzing teacher behavior in classrooms, and the results are encouraging; however, these research findings have not provided a foolproof list of "dos" and "don'ts" for running a classroom. Instead, research has provided a broad base of information from which essential characteristics of teachers and general principles of effective classroom management have been extrapolated. The research findings indicate that if teachers possess certain essential personal characteristcs and scientifically, artistically, and consistently apply effective principles of classroom management, then most discipline problems can be prevented or resolved (Good and Brophy, 1987).

The purpose of this book is fourfold: (1) to describe teacher characteristics, attitudes, and conditions necessary to manage classrooms and teach discipline; (2) to identify fundamental generic principles of effective classroom management and discipline; (3) to suggest teacher behaviors and activities that demonstrate successful application of these principles; and (4) to demonstrate how planning for teacher and student behavior can prevent and resolve management and discipline problems.

Part One identifies teacher characteristics and attitudes that are essential to effective application of principles of classroom management. Essential teacher attitudes are identified and activities provided that will assist the preservice or beginning teacher with refinement and acquisition of those attitudes. The key to effective management is prevention, and Part Two emphasizes the importance of planning for behavior and suggests teacher behaviors that prevent management and discipline problems. Part Three suggests behaviors that maintain the effectively managed classroom and teach discipline. Part Four summarizes principles of effective management and discipline and helps teachers plan for preventing and resolving management and discipline problems.

Successfully managing classrooms and teaching discipline is no easy task, but effective teachers do it at least 180 days a year. So can you.

Many thanks to a host of teachers and students who have experimented with these ideas and methods in workshops and classes. Special thanks to those who contributed personal experiences and materials: M. Valbrun-Pope, H. Nixon, J. Martin, B. Salomatoff, S. McCrimmon, F. Calabrese, A. Zanasco, O. Thompson, S. Hamell Smith, B. Rieves,

K.E. Howell, S. Rogers, and others too numerous to list. I also appreciate the valuable suggestions provided by the manuscript reviewers: Charles P. Doyle, Peter Gilman, Mark Pitts, Francis Curtis, John H. Hoover, and Sidney R. Miller.

T.V. McQueen

PART
One

CREATING CONDITIONS ESSENTIAL TO EFFECTIVE MANAGEMENT AND DISCIPLINE

Some form of inappropriate student behavior is, unfortunately, a normal, everyday occurrence, even in well-managed classrooms. Therefore, prospective teachers need to understand and know how to apply principles of effective management and discipline.

Chapter 1 identifies philosophies of child development and defines and clarifies the concepts of management, discipline, and teacher power as used throughout the book. Fundamental to effective management and discipline and the effective use of power are certain personal qualities that teachers must possess. These essential teacher attitudes and characteristics are discussed in Chapter 2.

After completing Part One you should understand the concepts of management, discipline, and power. You should also understand those teacher attitudes essential to effective management and discipline; and, if necessary, you should develop a plan to acquire and enhance those characteristics.

Chapter
1

An Introduction to Management and Discipline

INTRODUCTION AND OBJECTIVES

How times have changed since our grandparents went to school! Today critics of American society lament that young people are rude to their parents and teachers, do not respect authority, and fail to learn self-discipline. Grandparents relate that when they got a spanking at school, they got another at home, and they allow that nowadays children are not disciplined at home or at school. Over the past 50 years Americans have participated in a world war, the Korean War, the Vietnam War, a cold war, and Operation Desert Storm, as well as wars on poverty and drugs. They have been a part of reversing Supreme Court decisions, liberating women, attempting to guarantee the civil rights of all citizens, developing a standard of living envied around the world, sending men to the moon, developing a school system for all students, and teaching everyone the right to dissent. In our grandparents' lifetime the concept of democracy has expanded; equality is no longer for just a privileged few. All segments of society are seeking and securing equal opportunity and equal justice. Demands of immigrants, minorities, citizens of lower socioeconomic status, and women have contributed to a sense of democratic living that cries out for a softer, kinder, gentler, more egalitarian, and more effective use of authority at all levels, in all institutions, and especially in our schools. Schools reflect the values and dreams of our national, state, and local communities. The American concept of democracy is no longer simply to provide educational opportunity for the majority, but for all students. All students now have recognized rights, which until recently could be and often were ignored. What our grandparents call lack of respect for our elders and authority in many cases may be resentment of the abuse and misuse of authority. The ambiance of American democracy has changed and continues to change. Students are no longer willing to accept the complete, unquestioned authority of stereotypical teachers nostalgically described in nineteenth-century fiction. Today teachers must move away from demanding, ordering, and punishing toward requesting, helping, and guiding students. The goal of this book is to help teachers manage classrooms and teach discipline in classrooms composed of a diverse mix of students from the total spectrum of mental ability, socioeconomic status, and ethnicity.

Effectively managing classrooms and teaching discipline encompass a major portion of a teacher's professional skills. These two functions require continuous acquisition of knowledge and the ongoing, never-ending modification and refinement of related skills. In addition to the infinite complexity of these functions, they can be highly controversial. There is no one universally accepted way to teach discipline and manage classrooms. In fact, there is a wide spectrum of opinion as to how these skills should be applied and for what purpose. Opinions range from the biblical pronouncement that "sparing the rod spoils the child" to the belief that striking a child is immoral.

However, a large body of research on child development and teaching and learning is making it possible to rid the teaching profession of discipline myths and to identify valid, reliable generic principles for effectively managing classrooms and teaching discipline. This book identifies those principles that are appropriate for use in both elementary and secondary schools and are essential to the effective management of classrooms and teaching discipline. The principles are derived from the research literature and reflect a wide range of philosophies of discipline and theories of child development. Some principles reflect bold humanism; others take into account the teacher's need and responsibility to manage classrooms effectively. They are an eclectic collection of fundamental guidelines that have a basis in research and practice, are consistent with many approaches to discipline, and appear to be essential to any effectively managed classroom in which students learn self-discipline. Suggestions for implementing these essential principles represent a wide variety of methods selected from research findings, discipline models, and the experiences of the author and a host of teachers.

After completing chapter 1 the preservice or beginning teacher will be able to:

describe three interpretations of child development,

tell how each interpretation of child development influences how teachers manage classrooms and teach discipline,

define and list kinds of teacher power,

explain why the use of power is an important characteristic of philosophies of discipline,

define management and discipline, and

tell why the principles in this book are considered essential to management and discipline.

MANAGEMENT AND DISCIPLINE

The critics of American schools are not alone in their concern about behavior of the young. Public opinion polls indicate that discipline in schools is a major concern of all segments of our society—parents, teachers, the business community, and even students. What is discipline anyway? The term *discipline* is often used in referring to teacher behavior intended to "keep students in line," to implement consequences for failure to behave appropriately, and to enforce rules. This concept denotes teacher control and regimentation, which the public wants and demands, and it is often confused with punishment.

Punishment is based on the notion of inflicting harm or inducing pain and is generally conceived as an unpleasant, painful consequence aimed at suppressing inappropriate behavior. It can be denial of privileges, reprimands, scoldings, threats and suspensions, or even physical hurt. Physical punishment is not an infrequent occurrence in American schools. A report of the U.S. Department of Education (1988) states that in one school year more than one million students received physical punishment for misbehavior. Many educators believe corporal punishment belongs in a museum, yet it never quite dies as an educational issue. School personnel who advocate and use physical punishment argue that because many parents use this form of punishment, students are used to and respond only to this type of punishment; however, research findings clearly suggest that using corporal punishment as a method of managing classrooms has far more disadvantages than advantages.

The most effective teacher behaviors aimed at altering, suppressing, and stopping inappropriate student behavior are disciplining behaviors, but they do not involve causing pain or attacking self-esteem (Weber, et al., 1983). Instead, they are directed at helping students learn self-discipline and manage their own behavior. In this text discipline refers to a broad range of teacher and student behaviors aimed at enabling students to behave in appropriate ways. The purpose of disciplining behaviors is to help students, not to inflict emotional or physical pain. It should be noted that punishment may temporarily stop unacceptable behavior, but it may not help students find more acceptable ways of behaving.

A term frequently used by school personnel when they refer to classroom behavior of teachers and students is *classroom management*. Recent studies conducted by researchers at the National Institute for Research on Teaching (NIRT) and others have focused on classroom management as directing and orchestrating all elements of a classroom. Management sees to it that the business at hand—in our case, teaching and learning—can be carried out. Research findings indicate that successful managers control in purposeful ways their own behavior, which in turn influences students to behave in appropriately designated ways. The focus of effective managers is on teacher behaviors that influence and control the classroom environment in a positive fashion. Successful classroom managers are aware that their own behavior is a potential source of influence for both appropriate and inappropriate student behavior, and therefore they model the behavior they expect of students.

Effective classroom managers not only manage their own behavior and that of students in positive ways, they also manage other essential elements of the overall classroom. They effectively control room arrangements, the time allocated for teaching, methods of instruction, expectations of students, rules, materials, and so on. They orchestrate the interactions and relationships of all aspects of the classroom. They contrive to get along, ensure appropriate behavior, and direct success in whatever is needed. Teachers may be able to manage materials, time, and student movement and enforce rules by using threats and punishment; however, the ultimate goal of successful managers is not simply to manage classrooms but to create conditions that enable students to manage their own behavior and become self-disciplined.

Ideally, students should have acquired motivation to learn self-control and appropriate human relations before they come to school. If this ideal condition existed, directing students to practice appropriate behavior and punishing inappropriate behavior would be un-necessary. Unfortunately, human nature requires that teachers teach discipline and sometimes punish inappropriate student behavior. One can readily see why the concept of effective management includes teaching self-discipline.

You already know there are strong differences of opinion as to how children should be reared, how classrooms should be managed, and how discipline should be taught. For example, the local shopping mall is often the stage where vivid scenes of personal drama between angry, frustrated, bewildered, embarrassed children and parents are acted out. The child flails arms and legs, cries, screams, and rejects parental demands or consolation. In turn the parent ignores, consoles, cajoles, or threatens in whispers and shouts and may finally, in desper-ation or anger, strike the screaming youngster. Whatever action is taken by the parent, it is condemned and applauded by members of the audience. Some bystanders remark, "That child needs to be taught a lesson;" others say, "That child needs a good hard spanking;" and still others say, "Poor kid, how awful to be hit, especially in public." It seems most people agree on the need for teaching and learning disci-pline, but there is little agreement as to how this should be done.

PHILOSOPHIES OF CHILD DEVELOPMENT

Interpretations of child development by psychologists serve as the cognitive basis for a wide range of approaches to management and discipline. Three widely accepted interpretations are: (1) children are intrinsically motivated to develop their potential; (2) children are shaped and molded by external forces from the environment and other powers; and (3) children develop and are shaped through inter-actions between their intrinsic motivation and external forces.

Wolfgang and Glickman (1980) have labeled teachers according to their interpretation of how children develop. Teachers who believe that children, if given the chance, will be internally motivated to learn and behave appropriately are labeled noninterventionists. They be-lieve in supportive environments where students are free to express themselves and become unique, fully functioning adults. Noninterven-tionist teachers create classroom conditions that lead and guide stu-dents to behave in appropriate ways. They believe students want to succeed and that when given the right conditions, they will succeed.

Their view is that if schools were exciting, challenging, rewarding places, kids wouldn't try so hard to be absent, or be dumb or tough. Something says they would work harder, act nicer, and learn more if school were meeting their needs, awakening their minds, and touching their hearts.

Teachers who believe that children need and must have external control to develop their potential are labeled interventionists. Interventionist teachers intervene to control, manage, and discipline. They believe students must be watched, supervised, and corrected, and that students need rules, regulations, and consequences to force and condition them to behave. Interventionists see behavior and behavior changes as the result of external stimulation, and they discount inner motivation, which is extolled by the noninterventionists. The interventionists' philosophy is based on the behaviorist theory of B. F. Skinner, which is the basis for behavior modification discipline models.

Teachers who believe a child develops through interactions between internal motivation and external control are called interactionalists. They believe problems can be resolved by mutual teacher-student action, and that it may be necessary for the teacher to play many roles, such as listener, clarifier, rule maker and enforcer. Interactionalists believe that students and teachers share responsibility for behavior and that both must be actively involved in developing appropriate actions for learning and acquiring discipline. More teachers probably behave as interactionalists and interventionists than as non-interventionists. (See Form 1.1.)

Form 1.1   PHILOSOPHIES OF CHILD DEVELOPMENT AND TEACHER CONTROL

Noninterventionist	Interactionalist	Interventionist
Least direct control by teacher	Mixture of teacher control and student self-control	Most direct control by teacher
Most student self-control		Least student self-control
Example: Ginott model	Example: Glasser model	Example: Canter model

Over the last 25 years research in psychology, sociology, and teaching and learning has made it possible to develop principles of management and discipline that support each of these interpretations of child development. In addition, a number of management and discipline models have been developed by one or more ardent supporters of each philosophy.

For example, *Assertive Discipline: A Take-Charge Approach for Today's Educator* (1976) by Lee and Marlene Canter is one of the most widely used interventionist models. The Canters believe that teachers should insist on appropriate student behavior. They indicate teachers must be confident of their right and ability to secure and maintain order and must be persistently positive in their relations with students. Teachers must identify and communicate expectations of students, and in so doing they should not be hostile but simply assertive. Teachers should follow through on promises instead of making threats, and when they deal with student behavior, they should use statements of expectations, indicate consequences, and remind students why their action is necessary. The Canters give many suggestions for assertiveness, communicating expectations, and consistency.

The prime example of the interventionist approach to discipline is behavior modification. There are many models of this approach and many adaptations of its basic principle of operant conditioning. More will be said about the behavior modification approach in Chapter 5.

Dr. Haim Ginott's philosophy of human relations was popular in the 1960s and 1970s. His ideas were popularized by the media and are still considered keys to positive human interactions. Many "common-sense" suggestions for positive approaches to discipline and self-esteem are based on Ginott's books, *Between Parent and Child* (1965), *Between Parent and Teenager* (1969), and *Teacher and Child* (1972). Ginott believed the most important ingredient in discipline is the teacher's own self-discipline. The second most important is sending "sane" messages to students. "Sane" messages speak to the situation at hand, not to the student's self. He also believes that teachers should model the behavior they want from students and that the best teachers help students build self-esteem. Ginott's writings reflect the noninterventionist philosophy and give specific examples of its implementation. Other well-known models of the non-interventionist philosophy are Thomas Gordon's *Teacher Effectiveness Training* (1974) and *I'm OK—You're OK* by Thomas Harris (1969).

The ideas of psychiatrist William Glasser, set forth in his book *Schools Without Failure* (1969), are widely accepted as workable, practical approaches to developing discipline. Glasser believes that students are rational and can be reasoned with, but rules are necessary and must be enforced with reasonable consequences for both appropriate and inappropriate behaviors. Teachers who care about students will accept no excuses for bad behavior; they persist and never give up on students. They review rules and responsibilities and help students identify alternatives to bad behavior. Suggestions from Glasser's interactionalist model are widely used in many school systems. Rudolph Dreikurs' (1972) *Discipline Without Tears* is another well-known interactionalist model.

Finally, Jacob Kounin's research on classroom management outlined in *Discipline and Group Management in Classrooms* (1970) is not a behavior model but describes a system of teaching that encompasses classroom management. His research reveals that effective managers maintain an interesting curriculum environment and hold students accountable for their own behavior and learning. It also focuses on the teacher's ability to make smooth transitions between classroom activities and to maintain momentum and group alertness. Kounin says an effective manager is a "with it" teacher who is aware of everything that goes on in the classroom.

The central, if not singularly distinguishing, characteristic of each of these and other models is the philosophy inherent in each as to how teachers should use power to influence student behavior. The teachers' view of how their power can and should be used will affect, if not determine, their management and discipline methods. Because most of us already have some notion about how teachers should use power, let us look at the sources and importance of teacher power.

TEACHER POWER

There are many sources of teacher power—school boards, students, parents, teacher personality, and so on. State and local boards of education give teachers the authority to plan, set goals for learning, and teach in accordance with state and local guidelines. In order to teach and motivate students to learn there must be order in the classroom; therefore, teachers are given authority, within legal and moral guidelines, to teach and secure and maintain orderly classrooms. Wise and prudent use of conferred authority is central to the teacher's role as leader in the classroom. The failure to use authority wisely and prudently can result in the failure to acquire power.

In spite of the knowledge that teachers are given authority to teach and maintain order, one of their biggest fears is that they will not have the power to use the authority given them. Many teachers are powerless to influence student behavior. Activities that occur in powerless teachers' classrooms are determined by students. Research findings indicate that in some classrooms, particularly at the junior and senior high school levels, there sometimes is a silent, implicit agreement between teachers and students to expect very little from each other. Students implicitly agree to permit the teacher to go through the motions of teaching, and the teacher implicitly agrees to go along with this understanding and not expect "too much" from the students. Researchers call this Horace's compromise (Sizer, 1984). Why would a teacher agree to such an arrangement? Perhaps because the teacher recognizes the lack of ability to enforce rules and procedures, to make curricular decisions and basically to carry on the business of teaching and learning. The compromise is a way of being allowed to continue in the teaching role. Other teachers fight back and refuse to compromise; some win the power struggle, and others lose.

Some teachers view power as a dirty word. Their concept of power is pushing kids around, using force, assuming the position that the teacher is always right. This concept of power is the misuse of authority. In truth, the stereotypical teacher who misuses authority has less power than the teacher who recognizes that if you have power it is often unnecessary to exercise authority.

Wolfgang and Glickman (1980) note that noninterventionist teachers make minimal use of power in the classroom, and interventionists use power more freely. Interactionalists use power more overtly than the noninterventionists and less overtly than the interventionists.

Sociologists, psychologists, and teachers recognize that there are not only varied approaches to the use of power but that there are also different kinds of power: legitimate, expert, attractive, reward, and coercive (French and Raven, 1960). Legitimate power is similar to authority in that it allows the teacher to make decisions and do things because that is the teacher's prerogative. The teacher decides such things as the time allowed for completion of assignments, when and where to go on a field trip, when to move on to the next topic, when to convene groups, and so on. This official position is recognized by the students, and because *the teacher is the teacher* she or he can make these decisions. Legitimate power is enhanced through the acquisition of other kinds of power. If the teacher possesses legitimate power only, students tend to question the legitimacy of decisions even when the decision-making authority is legally conferred.

A second type of power is expert power. Teacher expertness creates power and enhances the exercise of authority. Teachers have this power because they possess superior knowledge and are seen as experts in their field. Teachers with expert power tend to believe they transmit important information to students. They view themselves as advocates of the intellectual endeavor and keepers of ideals and culture. They know a lot, they are smart, they enjoy talking about their subject, and they are enthusiastic!

Students in middle, junior high, and senior high schools may recognize, appreciate, and be influenced by expert power more than young children are. Muddling through content without sufficient knowledge and understanding to teach that content or giving misinformation will not go unnoticed by older students. Even in the early grades, teachers who are poor spellers, use poor grammar, and write poor compositions will be found out by parents, peers, and many students. Any influence and respect teachers may have had because of their legitimate power and position will vanish because they are perceived as not qualified for the role. Teachers at all school levels are expected by virtue of their teaching license to be expert.

Another kind of power is influence derived from the nature of human relationships. This is often called attractive power and is the influence teachers acquire because they accept their students' individuality and understand human behavior. They are personable, likeable, and caring. Students tend to believe these teachers will tell the truth, help them if they need it, understand their foibles, and respect them. Teachers with attractive power are able to influence student behavior by appealing to the human dimension. Students accept teacher decisions without criticism or rebellion because they regard the teacher with respect and affection. They want to please the teacher because the teacher pleases them. Attractive power is especially effective with the young, although it also appeals to older students and even adults. Most teachers, especially in elementary schools, begin school with some attractive power because young students start the school year with a favorable disposition toward school and their teachers. Many teachers take this honeymoon period for granted and fail to nurture and reinforce student positive attitudes. Other teachers do not assume the honeymoon will last, and they purposely work at building positive human relationships. Noninterventionist teachers rely on attractive and expert power.

Reward power is the influence teachers have in acknowledging student accomplishments. Praise, the most common form of reward, genuinely and specifically targeted can be a powerful influence on students' desire to cooperate and behave properly. The power of rewards often depends on the attractiveness and expertness of the teacher. Praise from a scholarly teacher whom the students admire and respect is potentially a more powerful influence than praise from a teacher who is not especially admired, liked, or perceived as expert.

Coercive power is the opposite of rewards; it is the power to punish. Most teachers do not like to use coercive power because they recognize that punishment can diminish student compliance with teacher requests, increase resistance to teacher influence, and induce fear. Because actions that punish often interfere with learning, every effort should be made to use other forms of power. Reward and coercive power are used by interventionists and to some degree by interactionalists.

Power does not reside solely in teachers; students also have power and can influence teachers. They have legitimate rights and the power to reward and punish. For example, students "like" teachers who cooperate with their wishes, such as giving little or no homework or few tests, and they reward these teachers by being friendly, smiling, and cooperative. They punish teachers who fail to succumb to their demands by being unfriendly, unsmiling, and uncooperative (Brophy and Evertson, 1981). Instructors feel better about their performance and warmer toward students when students respond with nonverbal indications of interest than when students do not respond in positive ways. Students' disapproval of teachers can influence teachers to behave in ways that do not always enhance teaching and learning (Feldman and Prohaska, 1979). In addition to legitimate, reward, and coercive power, some students also have attractive and expert power. Even teachers sometimes seek approval of popular students, student leaders, academically talented students, and students of high socioeconomic status. Teachers who use their own power wisely are able to resist undesirable student influence from any source for any reason.

SUMMARY

This book is devoted to selected fundamental, generic principles of management and teaching discipline appropriate for use in both elementary and secondary schools. These principles are derived from the research and teacher education literature and reflect at least three interpretations of child development. Some principles imply that children are molded and shaped by external forces; others imply that internal forces shape student behavior; and others suggest the importance of both internal and external control. Because no one interpretation of child development explains the development of all children and no one method or approach to management and teaching discipline works all the time, with all students, in all situations, the principles are an eclectic collection of ideas that range from caring about students to writing rules.

The key concepts used in the remaining chapters are defined in the following way: Classroom management is directing and orchestrating all elements in the classroom environment to create the conditions necessary for teaching and learning. Management includes discipline and punishment.

Discipline, the orderly conduct and training that develops self-control by both students and teachers, is the heart of management. A major purpose of management is to teach self-discipline.

Punishment, which is sometimes necessary in managing classrooms, consists of penalties aimed at stopping inappropriate behavior. It should be used only when all other methods of eliminating inappropriate behavior have been utilized and have failed.

In this chapter you have also learned that the authority to teach and manage classrooms is conferred by state and local school authorities, and the use of power is central to any philosophy or plan for managing classrooms and developing discipline. Teachers and students can acquire and use several kinds of power. Two kinds of teacher power that are essential to effective management are expert and attractive power. Teachers who acquire expert and attractive power understand and exhibit attitudes that are essential to effective management. Chapter 2 describes these indispensable, essential attitudes and characteristics and provides suggestions for their acquisition.

QUESTIONS AND ACTIVITIES

1.1 Characterize the management and discipline philosophy of non-interventionists, interactionalists, and interventionists.

1.2   How does teaching discipline differ from managing a classroom?

1.3 What are the advantages and disadvantages of an eclectic approach to management and discipline?

1.4 Why are expert and attractive power so important to teachers?

1.5 List at least five ways teachers can acquire attractive power.

1.6 Give an example of teacher behavior that illustrates both management and discipline skills.

1.7 Discuss teacher behaviors you have observed which you believe were intended to develop student self-discipline.

1.8 Make a list of classroom behaviors that teachers have been given authority to perform.

1.9 Ask a local teacher (someone you know) about how he or she exercises authority and uses power in the classroom.

1.10 List some human relations techniques that might be seen as "attractive" by young students but not by students in the secondary schools.

1.11 From your knowledge of psychology, discuss reactions of students of all ages to unbridled use of authority and power by teachers.

1.12 Based on your own observations, list some ways teachers abuse their authority.

1.13 What is your philosophy of management and discipline? Are you a non-interventionist, an interventionist, or an interactionalist teacher?

REFERENCES

Brophy, J., and Evertson, C. (1981). *Student Characteristics and Teaching.* New York: Longman.

Canter, L., and Canter, M. (1976). *Assertive Discipline: A Take-Charge Approach for Today's Educator.* Los Angeles: Lee Canter and Associates.

Dreikurs, R., and Cassel, P. (1972). *Discipline Without Tears.* New York: Hawthorn.

Feldman, R., and Prohaska, T. (1979). "The Student as Pygmalion: Effect of Student Expectation on the Teacher." *Journal of Educational Psychology,* 71, pp. 485–493.

French, J., and Raven, B. (1960). "The Bases of Social Power." In Cartwright, D., and Zander, A., eds. *Group Dynamics: Research and Theory* (2nd ed.). Evanston, Il.: Row Peterson, p. 612.

Ginott, H. (1965). *Between Parent and Child.* New York: Avon Books.

——— (1969). *Between Parent and Teenager.* New York: Macmillan.

——— (1972). *Teacher and Child.* New York: Macmillan.

Glasser, W. (1969). *Schools Without Failure.* New York: Harper and Row.

Good, T., and Brophy, J. (1987). *Looking in Classrooms* (4th ed.). New York: Harper and Row.

Gordon, T. (1974). *T.E.T. Teacher Effectiveness Training.* New York: Holt, Rinehart and Winston.

Harris, T. (1969). *I'm OK—You're OK: A Practical Guide to Transactional Analysis*. New York: Harper and Row.

Kounin, J. (1970). *Discipline and Group Management in Classrooms*. New York: Holt, Rinehart and Winston.

Rogers, C. (1969). *Freedom to Learn*. Columbus: Charles E. Merrill.

Sizer, T. (1984). *Horace's Compromise*. Boston: Houghton-Mifflin.

Skinner, B. (1953). *Science and Human Behavior*. New York: Macmillan.

U.S. Department of Education (1988). *The Condition of Education* (1987 edition). Washington, D.C.: United States Printing Office.

Weber, W., Roff, L., Crawford, J., Robinson, C. (1983). *Classroom Management. Reviews of the Teacher Education and Research Literature*. Princeton, N.J.: Educational Testing Service, p. 34.

Wolfgang, C., and Glickman, C. (1980). *Solving Discipline Problems: Strategies for the Classroom Teacher*. Boston: Allyn and Bacon, pp. 11–15, 15–19.

Chapter
2
Acquiring Essential Teacher Attitudes

INTRODUCTION AND OBJECTIVES

The old and persistent myth that some people are born teachers recognizes what adults and children have known for centuries—that the personality of the teacher influences student behavior. In 1966, Fritz Redl, the renowned behavioral scientist, researcher and author, said, "For the job of establishing and maintaining good discipline the personality of the teacher is the most essential factor." Research done in the 1970s and 1980s confirms the importance of the teacher's personality. Good and Brophy (1987) in a summary of research findings list five personal attributes teachers *must* have in order to manage a classroom successfully. The researchers say teachers must:

1. have the respect and affection of the students;
2. be consistent and, therefore, credible and dependable;
3. assume responsibility for the students' learning;
4. value and enjoy learning and expect the students to do so, too;
5. communicate these basic attitudes and expectations to students and model them in behavior.[1]

---

[1]Reprinted with permission from T. Good and J. Brophy, *Looking in Classrooms*, (4th ed.), 1987, p. 228.

This chapter identifies principles of management and discipline associated with these essential teacher attributes. It also gives information and suggests activities designed to help the preservice or beginning teacher acquire and refine these essential attributes as well as utilize effective classroom management and discipline skills. Specifically the preservice or beginning teacher will be able to:

- list and give examples of teacher behaviors which demonstrate respect for students: consistency, dependability, and credibility; the value and joy of learning; responsibility for student learning; and the communication and modeling of these attributes and expectations to students;
- give reasons why the above attributes and behaviors are essential to successful classroom management; and
- demonstrate the above behaviors in a simulated or real classroom setting.

RESPECTING STUDENTS

One of the first principles teachers must apply when working with students is:

Effective classroom managers must respect students and have students' respect.

Respect is the honor or esteem we hold for ourselves and others. If we respect someone, we value that person and our behavior indicates that we do. We demonstrate respect through trust and the consideration we show others and ourselves. Psychologists indicate that trusting ourselves and others is a major part of respect. In order to respect we must be able to trust others to live up to reasonable expectations and treat others as we would have them treat us.

Some unknown author's mini-essay describes trust this way:

Trust Is
Trust is keeping your word.
Trust is the willingness to communicate.
Trust is being there.

Trust is consistency.

Trust is saying, "I understand; I believe in you; touch me; I care."

Trust is not needing to explain.

Trust is a responsibility.

Trust is a compliment.

Trust is an open feeling, being open.

Trust is a willingness to be vulnerable.

Trust is without fear.

Trust is a reciprocal thing.

Trust is knowing one another.

Trust is not taking advantage.

Trust is different things to different people.

Above all, Trust is risky.

Our relationships with the people who make up our world determine to some degree our personality. We learn from others who we are, what is expected of us, and how to please. Some of us are fortunate to have had kind, understanding, sensitive, caring, accepting, trusting persons in our world. They valued and trusted us and gave us consideration, honor, and esteem; and we learned to trust, honor, and respect those around us.

Others of us have not been fortunate enough to experience trusting, supporting relationships. A key person in our world may have been critical, unkind, selfish, unaccepting, and distrustful, which diminished our ego strength and self-esteem. Those of us who have lived with criticism often have to make a special effort to respect others as well as ourselves. This entails changing our own behavior. Changing attitudes and behaviors is not done easily or quickly. It requires recognition of the need to change, a willingness to change, a commitment, and a plan to bring about change. This is often a long, difficult process that may require professional assistance.

How do teachers behave who respect students? They listen! They really listen. They make an effort to get to know students. They keep their word. They believe in students. They respond to students in calm, reasonable ways. They see good things in students. They let students know they are appreciated. They give genuine praise, and they are genuine people. Teachers who are able to do these things have ego strength (Brophy and Putnam, 1978), which not only enables them to demonstrate respect for students but also stimulates students' respect for the teacher.

Ego strength encompasses self-confidence, the ability to stay calm in a crisis, and the ability to face difficulties with a problem-solving attitude. When you have ego strength, you are confident that you can discharge your duties and responsibilities; you believe in yourself, and you behave as if you know what you are doing—and you do. You do not believe students are "out to get you," and you are not psychologically "threatened." You do not perceive student misbehavior as deliberate and deliberately acted out in your classroom, and you are not afraid. You have self-discipline and self-knowledge, and you are sure without being cocky. You exude the aura that you have met with adversity and bested it. When you have ego strength, you respect yourself and you are able to respect students.

Teachers who respect students are easily and readily recognized by students and others. One student teacher described her supervising teacher in the following way:

> My supervising teacher had from the very start of the school year gained the respect and admiration of all students she had come in contact with. She had established a good rapport with them, even those who had been considered problems by teachers of previous years or other classes.
>
> I have never heard her yell or scream at the class. She has learned to control the tone, pitch, inflection, and expression of her speaking voice to suit all situations. This is one of the most important techniques I have learned from her.

Another preservice teacher wrote:

> My supervising teacher was very effective, probably because from the first day of school the students knew the rules. . . . She was also a very warm teacher. One who understood the problems of sixth graders about to enter junior high school. The students wanted to learn from her because they knew she had an interest in them as individuals. She not only took an interest in students' school activities, but in their outside activities and in their home life. Students recognized her not only as a teacher, but as a friend.

Look at the teacher behaviors in Form 2.1. From your own experience and the information in this chapter list more teacher actions that show respect for students.

Teachers who are able to remain calm and reasonable in crisis situations are self-disciplined. They are not rude, vengeful, and punishing. They do not scream, become hysterical, or throw temper tantrums. They are not perpetually angry with students and the world, and they do not misuse the authority that comes with their position. A common label for teachers who misuse power and fail to respect

Form 2.1 SHOWING RESPECT

A Student's View

If you didn't think a teacher liked you and respected you, which of the following would make you more sure that he or she did?
1. Greeting you with a real smile and a cheerful hello.
2. Inviting you to tell what you think about an idea or problem.
3. Listening to your side of the story.
4. Laughing with you and other students when funny things happen.
5. Taking an interest in your hobbies or other things you do outside the home.
6. Being careful not to embarrass you in front of other students by using ridicule such as "Imagine a big boy like you doing that," or pointing up your weaknesses such as "You have the lowest average in the room" or "If it weren't for you, we would have won the contest."
7. Being careful not to punish the entire class when one student is at fault.
8. Writing a note or telephoning when you are sick.
9. Letting your parents know when you do something especially good.
10. Letting you know she or he didn't think you were bad when she or he did not approve of your behavior.

---

students is the authoritarian teacher. The degree of authoritarianism displayed by teachers varies. A continuum exists with regard to all personality traits, and no two teachers express their authoritarian tendencies in the same way. In the most comprehensive review to date of research literature on the authoritarian personality and behavior, Crow and Bonney (1975) describe the authoritarian person as

> . . . weak, threatened, insecure, prejudiced, ethnocentric, conventional, moralistic, power oriented, superstitious, rigid, dogmatic, and sadomasochistic.[2]

They also say authoritarian teachers tend to view the classroom and their position as sources of almost unlimited power. They tell students in various ways, "You do this because *I say so*." They view students as objects to be bullied and manipulated. This attitude is communicated in subtle or overt ways but is always present. Authoritarian teachers place an inordinately high value on order, routine, and discipline. They tend to view minor rules and procedures as being as important as the curriculum content. These rules may be as inconsequential as

---

[2]Reprinted with permission from M. Crow and M. Bonney, "Recognizing the Authoritarian Personality Syndrome in Educators," *Phi Delta Kappan*, 57(1), p. 41.

putting one's name in a special place on a paper, how to sit in one's chair, and how to march out of the room. These authoritarian teachers also tend to be moralistic and conventional, and they might be described as living a good, clean life. They are able to convince people they are strong and capable, but underneath the tough veneer they may be weak and insecure.

> They present themselves to their own bosses in a very different way from the way they are around employees or students. Whereas, by his principal, an authoritarian teacher might be described as subservient and respectful, his students are more likely to describe him as disrespectful, harsh and punitive.[3]

It should be noted that effective teachers behave in an authoritarian manner when they perceive the need for direct guidance or intervention. Mild directives, mild desists, requests, and quiet, firm commands can be called authoritarian actions. The authoritarian teachers described here misuse power and are preoccupied with establishing unquestioned control of students. Teachers should be cautioned about authoritarian behavior and at the same time be encouraged to give directions and make requests and interventions with firmness and authority. Remember, on a continuum of authoritarian behavior the teacher should strike a workable balance between being the authoritarian teacher described by the researchers and a wimp who is ignored by students.

A preservice teacher described an overly authoritarian teacher she vividly remembered in the following way:

> The teacher I most vividly remember taught English in eleventh grade. Although I considered Mr. C. a human being, that's not the way I felt he treated "us," the class. He had the attitude that he was the teacher and we were the pupils. There was some vast difference between the two which he never bothered to explain.
>
> Mr. C. never seemed very happy. He seemed to resent the fact that he was teaching at all. He rarely cracked a smile or ever told us a joke. I can't remember him ever telling us about a hobby he might have had.
>
> When a sentence was written on the board, in just a matter of seconds, I could diagram it, and tell which words were the nouns, verbs, etc. and why. Most of the class did not have that background and neither did Mr. C. When there was a discrepancy about some sentence on the board, which happened almost immediately after school started, I explained to

---

[3]M. L. Crow, personal communication, Feb. 27, 1990.

him how I thought it should be. When I was proved right, it was World War III from that moment on. When something specific was brought up he wasn't sure about, he often said, "Is that alright with you, Miss X?"

When grades came out at the end of the six-week term, I had a 98 average and I got a B in the class. When I went to him to talk about "our" problem he simply refused to discuss the matter. No matter what average I got he always gave me one grade lower. Needless to say I quit trying. By the end of the year I was lucky to have a C average, over all.

Form 2.2 BEHAVIOR CHECKLIST

Behaviors that show respect	Behaviors that show lack of respect
1. I truly listen to others. ____	1. I ignore others. ____
2. I have a warm, calm, accepting voice. ____	2. I have a sharp, critical, impatient voice. ____
3. I ask and request. ____	3. I demand. ____
4. I let others talk and express opinions. ____	4. I interrupt others. ____
5. I genuinely praise. ____	5. I give phony praise. ____
6. I refrain from criticizing. ____	6. I criticize freely. ____
7. I remember "good things" others do. ____	7. I remember "bad things" others do. ____
8. I remind others of their "good behavior" and accomplishments. ____	8. I remind others of their "bad behavior" and failures. ____
9. I hold reasonable and realistic expectations of others. ____	9. I hold unreasonable and unrealistic expectations of others. ____
10. I recognize and appreciate strengths of others. ____	10. I recognize and delight in weaknesses of others. ____

It is often easier to recognize undesirable behavior in others than in ourselves. The checklist in Form 2.2 will help you recognize characteristics of your behavior. Be honest with yourself, and if possible ask someone who is close to you to confirm your perceptions. Research findings indicate that teachers indeed attribute student behavior to the students' personal characteristics, but they tend to attribute teacher behavior to factors external to their own personal characteristics. In other words, the teacher is critical because students need the criticism, not because the teacher has the need to criticize (Brophy and Rohrkemper, 1981). When you deal with unacceptable student behavior, be sure you separate that behavior from the student as an individual. Do not attack the student personally.

Excerpts from essays written by student teachers who were asked

to describe any management or discipline problems in their classrooms illustrate their perception of the sources of management and
discipline problems. Notice that they often attribute problems to students' personal characteristics and factors beyond the teacher's control, but there is also evidence of insight into the nature of some of the
problems.

Teacher 1

Immaturity is problem number one and the basis of most other problems.
School experience will probably be the best remedy for this, but there are
related problems which really stop me. These children seem to relish
stealing to aggravate, hitting and destroying others property. In a group of
twenty children, I'm aware of only one that at any time thinks of others in
a positive manner. It seems there is little time during the day for the
children to express themselves, and when they do, it is in the manner
described above.

Teacher 2

I have very bad discipline problems in my fourth grade class. All of the
bright children were pulled out and put into another class.

I have 26 boys in the class and only 10 girls. This is one of the main
reasons for the discipline problem. There are too many students in the
class to begin with, and the boys seem to constantly cause trouble in the
classroom. They don't listen to directions, they run around the room, they
don't stay in their seats, they don't finish their work, and they don't listen
to directions.

Also, these students have no respect for anyone. No punishment
bothers them, and they aren't afraid of anything. The boys think it is fun
to get in trouble. Even going to the principal's office doesn't bother them.

Teacher 3

I have a gripe about the schedule in general. Nothing is allowed and
everything is done. Lunch is most horrible. They [students] must line up,
no talking, and after they sit down the "witch (principal) comes on the
horn." The speaker is so loud it hurts my ears. It must affect the children.

Now that I have thoroughly given the system "what for," I'd like to
add that children bring problems from home. Some children come so
"hopped up" and antagonistic that you know plenty is going on. Usually,
after contact with the parents you discover that they too are antagonistic,
so all there is to do is take the pressure from the child as best you can and
still conduct the class. I have found that accepting feelings is the most
potent weapon against unacceptable behavior.

Teacher 4

John is the main cause of discipline problems in my class. He has many problems and is a hyperactive child. He constantly seeks attention, whether this attention is positive or negative. He continuously disrupts the class, makes the children laugh, threatens to beat them up, and pushes them around. You would never believe he is only eight years old. It is very hard to maintain good discipline in the class when John seeks attention, which is continuously. John is a discipline problem that needs long-range help. I am trying to help him by keeping him after school to help me and win his confidence. When he stays after school, he is a different person.

Teacher 5

The students are from varied backgrounds, many from low-income, underprivileged homes, which make for an atmosphere that gets out of hand frequently. These sixth graders hold no "fear" and very little respect for authority. If they want to sit in the middle of the floor and shout while a lesson is going on they just might do so. Take student A for an example: "typical" 11 year old, 5 ft. 10 in. tall and about 190 pounds!! When speaking to this child privately and discussing topics that interested her, she is just a doll; but regular classroom activity turns her into an outspoken, pouting "monster." There are several children with the same qualifications for monster. At first I just demanded respect because "I was the teacher." Later I realized it was much more effective to give these students the individual recognition they are striving for and they become much more cooperative.

Make a list of the causes of problems in these five classrooms as perceived by the student teachers. You can readily see that most problems are attributed to the nature of the students. Only teacher 3 attributes behavior problems to the school climate or atmosphere. Teachers 3, 4, and 5 allude to teacher behaviors which they believe might be helpful, but all five apparently believe that behavior problems are primarily caused by students' cultural and economic backgrounds and personality traits. Any possible connection between students' behavior and their own behavior appears to have been given no thought.

Dealing with Fear

A teacher who is respectful of others is a strong teacher—one who is not afraid to permit differences of opinion, to listen, to reason with and trust students. But all of us know that not all teachers are strong and respect students and that not all students are reasonable and respect teachers. In truth, a few schools in some parts of the United States may not be safe for teachers and students. The foregoing discussion of ego strength and respecting students is not intended to minimize the dangers some few teachers face on a daily basis as they attempt to deal with students who do not respect themselves, other students, or their teachers. Neither is the intent to imply that teachers who work in dangerous settings should not be fearful. However, some teachers are unnecessarily fearful, and students intuitively sense when teachers are afraid, and they use that fear to destroy teacher authority and ego strength.

Fear enters the classroom because of students' needs to acquire power. They strive to assert themselves as human beings, and they test adult authority because they want independence and control of their own actions and lives. As students continually push to acquire control, teachers must guard their authority, strive to influence student behavior, and be aware of their own fears. When students express dislike, teachers fear rejection and the loss of attractive power. When students are unmotivated and refuse to learn, teachers fear their expert power has evaporated. When rewards and punishment become ineffective they become overly restrictive or overly permissive and they are afraid.

Fear is insidious. We are afraid to talk about our fears, for fear our colleagues and superiors will know. We mask our fears through apathy, arrogance, and hostility. If fear pervades, respect vanishes, enthusiasm dies, everything we do is mechanical, and the joy of teaching and learning is gone. Fear destroys attitudes conducive to effective management, and teachers coerce and herd students instead of guide them. Classrooms become filled with confusion and a lack of direction instead of purposefulness and interest. Little learning is accomplished in a fear-filled classroom.

Students can be uncannily sensitive to teachers' fears and clearly schooled in how to use those fears to their advantage. Pickhardt (1978) interviewed students in detention halls and in-school suspension rooms to determine strategies students use to intimidate teachers. The following are some of the strategies he found.

1. Students find out what teachers want, and they do the opposite. For example, if the teacher wants them to participate in class, they keep silent. If the teacher wants them to sit up straight, they slouch and slump. If the teacher wants their

approval, they withdraw it. They use nonverbal facial and body language as a powerful weapon to induce teacher insecurity and fear.

2. Students use teacher interpretations of student behavior to their advantage. For example, staring the teacher down and letting the teacher wonder what is motivating the stare, or, when the teacher demands that students look him or her in the eye, they refuse, but listen and "fool" the teacher.

3. Students control a teacher's behavior through the volume of their voices. Loud voices demand prompt attention; low voices suggest secrets and conspiracies. In addition, when students respond in inaudible voices, the teacher feels forced to ask the students to repeat their responses.

4. When students' speech is purposely unclear, rapid, slurred, or mumbled, teachers must respond by ignoring, interpreting, or asking what was said; and the student cannot be blamed for not responding.

5. Students refuse to respond to the teacher's questions or give faulty information. For example, a teacher does not know the name of each student (this happens in large schools) and stops a student from running in the hall; the student gives the teacher a fake name, incorrect home room, and so on. This places the teacher at the mercy of his or her own ignorance.

6. Students manipulate the teacher to make conditional threats and issue demands such as, "If you open your mouth again, I will. . . . ," and when the conditions are not met, the teacher must "put up" or "back down." This strategy is most effective if used in front of the entire class.

7. Students make a scene, such as throwing a tantrum, to draw attention to themselves and then to the teacher, who is expected to "do something." Teachers become wary of students who make scenes and are very careful how they relate to those students.

8. Students put the teacher down with statements that show they do not hold the teacher in high regard. For example, they may use nicknames or say "yes, ma'am" to a man or "no sir" to a woman, and they may verbalize about the boring and repetitive work.

9. Students who resist teacher authority have excuses that will check out as valid or excuses that cannot be checked out. For

example, students do not have their work because "it was stolen," or they have family problems, or they did not understand.

10. Students use differences in physical appearance, and sexual and racial differences between students and teachers to exploit teachers. For example, students wear in class dark glasses that conceal their eyes and nourish the teacher's suspicion and distrust. Students of the opposite sex will make casual, covert, and even overt sexual suggestions to teachers. Students use racial differences to make teachers feel "different," guilty, ignorant, uncaring, and so on.

11. Threatening teachers with physical violence is the most powerful action students can take to induce fear. For example, students tell the teacher, "My friends will take care of you," "Watch your step," "I know what kind of car you drive," or "My parents will beat me if I don't pass." And one single, simple act of physical violence threatens all the teachers in a school.

Pickhardt (1978) makes the following suggestions to teachers when they encounter threatening student behavior:

1. Accept the fact that you are afraid. Do not deny it and do not be ashamed. (See Form 2.3.)
2. Try to increase your contact with the students you fear and get to know them better. You may fear them less.
3. Try not to show your fears.
4. Do not become overly restrictive or overly permissive. Both strategies are self-defeating.

The students he interviewed gave these three guidelines:

1. Don't back away—this shouts out to everyone that you are afraid.
2. Don't back down—this shouts out that you can be forced to act out of fear.
3. Don't fight back—this shouts out that you are fighting fear by fighting the student.[4]

---

[4]Pickhardt, Carl E. "Fear in the Schools? How Students Make Teachers Afraid," *Educational Leadership*. Nov. 1978, pp. 107–112. Reprinted with permission of the Association for Supervision and Curriculum Development. Copyright © 1978 by the Association for Supervision and Curriculum Development. All rights reserved.

Form 2.3 BEHAVIORS THAT TELL STUDENTS TEACHERS ARE AFRAID

1. Surrounds himself or herself with an iron wall
2. Blames without investigation
3. Treats students with disdain
4. Injects personal prejudices into relations with students
5. Is hostile to ideas not compatible with his or her own.
6. Treats students as objects or infants
7. Never admits a mistake
8. Disregards students' feelings
9. Threatens students
10. Fails to keep promises
11. Gets irritated with complaints
12. Uses certain students for scapegoats

Many of these behaviors may be demonstrated by authoritarian teachers, but not all teachers who are fearful are authoritarian.

BEING CONSISTENT, CREDIBLE, AND DEPENDABLE

A second principle of classroom management and discipline is:

> Effective managers must be consistent, credible, and dependable.

Credibility is fundamental to a teacher's ability to use management skills, to prescribe effectively behaviors that enhance discipline, and to impose penalties. Students must have confidence that teachers will do what they need to do and will do what they say (Good and Brophy, 1987). A teacher must be believed.

To acquire credibility, teachers should be consistent in enforcing rules and procedures. This does not mean consistently meting out the same penalty for the same offense to all offenders or even to the same offender. Settings in which inappropriate behavior occurs vary, and so do a student's motivations, needs, and characteristics. Therefore, a penalty may vary, but there must be consistent enforcement of the rule. For example, in enforcing a rule about hitting others, a student who frequently hits others for no apparent reason and one who hits another in reaction to being "called a name" might be given two different penalties, but in both instances the rule is enforced. When the same teacher only occasionally enforces rules, sometimes ignores the rule infractions, or simply threatens to enforce rules, some students "get away" with inappropriate behavior for which others are penalized. This is quickly seen as "unfair," and as a result students will resist a teacher's effort to enforce any rule.

Teachers who inconsistently enforce rules often make empty threats. Any threat needs to be carefully considered before it is made. Older students are more likely to "take you up on it" than young students, but the young also learn that you are a paper tiger. A threat is a curious thing; it is a promise, and it can also be a dare. When teachers make statements such as "I dare you to do that," or "if you do, we'll see who is in control" or "who is best," or "I promise you I will," the message is "I want you to be afraid to do this." Many students "take teachers up" on threats to see how insecure teachers really are and to expose them as bluffers. Credible and dependable teachers refrain from threatening students; they know the potentially dangerous effects of threatening. If a threat is made, that decision should be made with calm deliberation. All possible student responses should be considered. A threat made under stress, on the spur of the moment, can prove embarrassing or disastrous for the teacher, not the student. Even "innocent" or "reasonable" threats can backfire.

Consider all possible consequences of the teacher's behavior in the following anecdote, which actually took place in a California junior high English class.

> Mr. J. observed a rash of note passing between students, particularly between the girls. He asked for the students' attention and asked them to stop the note passing. It continued over the next few days. Finally, fed up and frustrated, he said, "The very next note I see passed in this classroom, I will read in front of the class."

What are some possible results of this threat? What actually happened to Mr. J. was that the note passing stopped for a day or two. Then he saw one girl pass a note to another across the aisle. He stopped teaching, walked to the girls and said, "OK! Remember what I said about passing notes? Give me the note." They handed it to him and he walked back to the front of the class as he unfolded the paper. One glance and he was stunned, but he read, "Mr. J.'s fly is undone." The class disintegrated into total bedlam; his trousers fly really was undone. He managed to close his fly, blushed, tried to restore order, and vowed to never make another threat.

Another facet of teacher credibility is the teacher's consistent interpretation of acceptable student behavior. If students learn that "No getting out of seats without permission" really means "No horsing around and running," students will get out of their seats without permission; when the teacher really expects them not to get out of their seats without permission, students react with hostility and resentment. Students believe the rule doesn't mean what it says. Avoid saying "Absolutely no talking," if it comes to mean, "Don't be too loud or I will punish you." Teacher credibility gives students something they rely on. When students believe you mean what you say and will act accordingly, they tend to "test the limits" of their behavior less because the limits are known. When teachers carefully consider their expectations of students and consistently communicate these expectations, credibility is enhanced.

In addition, credible teachers cannot be both Dr. Jekyll and Mr. Hyde. Consistency in the teacher's outlook and frame of mind eliminates the effects of a mercurial personality, which might be consistent in rule enforcement, expectations, rewarding, and penalizing, but which on occasion does these things with a vengeance and on another with benevolence. (See Form 2.4.)

Form 2.4 CONSISTENCY, CREDIBILITY, AND DEPENDABILITY

A Student's View

If you didn't think a teacher was consistent, which of the following would make you more sure of that teacher's consistency, dependability, and credibility? Can you add other suggestions?
1. Following through on promises.
2. Helping you when you really need help.
3. Admitting she or he made a mistake in information, judgement, and so on.
4. Administering appropriate penalties when needed.
5. Not resorting to mass punishment when she or he does not know the real culprits.
6. Not playing favorites.
7. Always expecting you to follow rules and do your work.
8. Responding to your signals that you are unhappy.
9. Not making threats.
10. Letting you know it is all right to move about occasionally if you have good reason and do not disturb others.

Teachers at all levels of schooling should recognize that credibility and dependability are essential to successful classroom management.

Young children as well as adolescents and adults are quick to recognize inconsistencies in what teachers say and do.

ASSUMING RESPONSIBILITY FOR LEARNING

A third principle of classroom management and discipline is:

Effective classroom managers accept responsibility for student learning.

One primary purpose of schooling is academic learning. Teachers who accept responsibility for students' learning believe their behavior and that of students can be constructively directed to learning and is attributable to factors over which they have some control. They recognize that the potential to control behavior outcomes lies within themselves rather than in outside factors over which they have no control. They believe that effort invested in a task and the level of success are predictability related. Responsible teachers actively instruct students and do not rely on passive supervision of student assignments. They also monitor seatwork or other independent learning activities for understanding, accuracy, and completion of work. Some teachers sit at their desks, grade papers, prepare lessons, or even write letters when students work independently; but teachers who feel a sense of responsibility for learning determine whether students need assistance, and they give help when needed, individually and in groups. Active involvement in instructing in some fashion is a characteristic of responsible teachers.

Teachers who assume responsibility for students' learning believe their students can learn and that they are capable of teaching their students, even the lower achievers. They give appropriate feedback, and they know the levels of student achievement; this enables them to pursue realistic instructional goals and see to it that all students experience success. They are serious about teaching and at the same time maintain a supportive learning environment. They do not lower their standards for unmotivated students or allow the fast learners and talented to languish on their past achievements. They have standards for the academically weak and do not allow them to founder in their lack of achievement. They challenge students to broaden their knowledge and sharpen their skills, and they do not ignore students' incompetence or failure to do assignments. (See Form 2.5.) Responsible teachers do not sacrifice student learning; nor do they abdicate their responsibility for student learning to obtain the approval of students or parents. They do not compromise their position by letting students determine goals and standards. They hold students accountable.

Form 2.5 TEACHER BEHAVIOR THAT INDICATES RESPONSIBILITY FOR STUDENT LEARNING

1. I plan for daily and long-range teaching.
2. I use content and make assignments my students find interesting.
3. I help students make "connections" between school learning and life.
4. I help students make "connections" with past learning.
5. I hold students accountable.
6. I teach at levels students can understand.
7. I make an effort to assist each student.
8. I hold realistic expectations for students.
9. I believe that all students can learn.
10. I expect good things. Students (and others) tend to live up to expectations of significant others.

If you answer "no" to any question, make plans to change that behavior!

The following descriptions by preservice student teachers give examples of teachers' behaviors which demonstrate responsibility for student learning. List the behaviors in each vignette which show responsibility for student learning and those which show a lack of responsibility. (See Form 2.6.)

Teacher 1

The teacher I best remember throughout my 14 years of schooling was my Spanish IV teacher in high school. She was very pleasant to talk with, kept a good air with her students, and knew what she was talking about.

Spanish class seemed to be the only class I looked forward to. I wasn't one to go and waste the hour. The teacher varied the class from day to day, working on different types of Spanish studies. She showed much personal concern for all of the students and always kept everyone busy with what she was teaching. She wasn't the type that embarrassed the student or kept him after school for not doing his homework. She kidded around about the problem, but you knew the assignment was to be learned by next time.

The most pleasant part about her class was that she was so cultured that she always added highlights that had reference to the lesson even though they were not directly related. This gave the students a wide view of the matter. I feel that a lot of my previous teachers didn't know what they were talking about. They taught directly from the book. It takes much more than a book to teach and teach well.

Teacher 2

I was in seventh grade and had never been very interested in science, but had always made good grades in the course. When I went to my first science class, I found Mrs. Y. was the teacher. She was demanding in what she expected of you, but it was never impossible. She made science fun and interesting for the whole class.

When we dissected pigs, she was right there beside us. When we used microscopes or experimented with chemicals, she was always as involved as we were.

We had a science fair at school that year, and everyone had to prepare an exhibit for their final grade. I was really stuck for a topic, but I found I could talk easily to Mrs. Y., and she was always very helpful and considerate. As a result of her encouragement and genuine interest in me and my project, I received an Honorable Mention from the Science Fair and "A" in her science class.

Teacher 3

The teacher I most vividly remember would be my fifth grade instructor. She was a large woman, and as I remember, she was always eating in the class. She would put an assignment on the board and then make her way to the cafeteria and food. She would return with a dish and a piece of bread, or a glass of ice.

Ms. R. gave a large amount of reading assignments during class. When we were not reading silently, we were asked to read aloud taking turns. Occasionally we had a movie, or a class trip. She was harsh and very lazy. Homework assignments were given in every subject. There was nothing exciting about going to school during those days.

Form 2.6 RESPONSIBILITY

A Student's View

If you didn't think your teacher assumed responsibility for teaching you, which of the following would make you think he or she did? Can you add suggestions to the list?
1. Finding out what your specific difficulties are in your inability to attack new words, solve word problems, or write an essay
2. Helping you find a systematic way to attack your difficulties
3. Centering some class activities around things you are interested in and problems you meet in daily living

4. Recognizing evidence of your improvement and the things you do well
5. Giving you chances to talk about your work and serve as a leader sometimes
6. Avoiding making you feel inferior by publicly comparing your work with that of other students
7. Helping you find at least one thing you do well
8. Providing assignments that you can successfully and correctly complete
9. Helping you develop skills that help you when the class plays games or has a social activity
10. Helping you find ways to contribute to group projects such as bringing in pictures and books, helping to arrange exhibits, and so on.

VALUING AND ENJOYING LEARNING

A fourth principle of classroom management and discipline is:

> Effective classroom managers value and enjoy learning themselves and expect students to do the same.

Many of the same behaviors that are exhibited by teachers who accept responsibility for student learning are also exhibited by teachers who value and enjoy learning. Perhaps those who value and enjoy learning themselves accept responsibility enthusiastically for student learning.

When teachers value learning, they present materials and assignments in ways that help students see school work as interesting and meaningful. They make connections with past learning and that which is yet to be accomplished. They present the rewards for work as satisfaction in knowing and using information and skills. They make no apologies for assignments and do not present work as something unpleasant that has to be done in order to play. They do not give homework assignments as penalties. They do not say, "When you have finished your assignment, you may do something for fun." Their behaviors do not imply that learning is unpleasant and school is a bore. They derive pleasure from teaching and seeing students learn (Good and Brophy, 1986).

Teachers who value and enjoy learning approach teaching with enthusiasm. Studies of enthusiastic teachers indicate that they convey commitment, excitement, and involvement with subject matter. Their lessons are stimulating and imaginative. Movement, gesture, variations in voice, animation, and eye contact are characteristic of enthusiastic teachers (Rosenshine and Furst, 1970). Eight indicators of high teacher enthusiasms are: (1) fast paced, uplifting, varied vocal delivery; (2) dancing, wide-open eyes; (3) frequent, demonstrative gestures; (4) varied, dramatic body movements; (5) varied, emotive facial expressions; (6) use of varied words, especially adjectives; (7) ready, animated acceptance of ideas and feelings; and (8) exuberant over-all energy level (Collins, 1976). These characteristics do not mean enthusiastic teachers must run around the room like cheerleaders. Enthusiasm can manifest itself in many ways. For example, English composition teachers who also write, art teachers who paint, drama teachers who act, and so on, display enthusiasm for learning. (See Form 2.7.)

Studies show that enthusiastic behavior can be learned. If you are enthusiastic but others are unaware of your enthusiasm, plan ways you can show your interest. Not only does enthusiasm indicate that teachers value and enjoy learning, but also teacher enthusiasm appears to affect student achievement positively.

Preservice teachers describe their teachers who valued and enjoyed learning in the following ways:

Teacher 1

I had Mr. B. for humanities when I was a junior in senior high school. He was an imposing man, short—about 5 ft. 4 in.—and stocky, with salt-and-pepper hair and a neatly trimmed moustache, well dressed in a conservative suit and tie.

I had taken humanities as a "light" course between my "heavy" classes of honors English, algebra II, American history, and advanced Latin. Music was my forte—and art, what could be difficult about that? It came as quite a shock to hear the stern-faced man in the front of the room talk about what would be expected of us: Projects? Reports? Exams? Pop quizzes? I groaned inwardly. What a year this was going to be!

But, as the year started, I realized I was wrong. We started with discussions of the ancient civilizations—Egyptians, Phoenicians, Babylonians, Greeks, Romans—their lives, art and culture. From there we turned to religion—what people believe, and how their beliefs have produced the world's bloodiest wars and most breathtaking works of art. We reviewed the new season's T.V. shows. We argued over the Academy Awards. We discussed architecture. We criticized art. We read books. We listened to music. We never knew quite what to expect when we walked into class, but it never failed to be interesting and exciting. Yes, there were projects and homework assignments, but they were challenging and fun ("With no more than four other people, prepare a pantomime for next week . . . "). Yes, we took notes in class too, but the only way I know that for sure is because I still have my notebook. I can remember sitting spellbound in third period, listening to Mr. B.'s lectures and fervently wishing class wouldn't end so soon.

I think perhaps the best quality of Mr. B. was his obvious love of learning. Though he was never unprepared for class sessions, he was flexible enough to allow for an occasional unexpected question to lead off in another direction, and he was always as excited as we were about the outcome of a project. Though he is "the teacher I most vividly remember," I would not say Mr. B. was really a teacher in the often used sense of the word. Instead, he explored and discovered the beauties of the arts together with us.

Teacher 2

My French teacher is the teacher I most vividly remember. She was a tall, slim lady with short hair, and she always looked very French. Her name was Mrs. N., and she was my teacher in high school. I remember her because she was an outstanding teacher.

Her classes were very interesting and lively; she would teach by the textbooks, but there was always something extra that made the class enjoyable. Not only did we learn about verbs, sentences, and everything about grammar, but we also learned about France. She would talk about French people, their food, their customs, way of life, and so on. She would also tell us all about the exciting places that we could visit if we ever had a chance to go to France.

One of the things that she really enjoyed was to show her students films of all her trips to parts of France and Paris. I learned a lot from her films, which helped me see how people live in other parts of the world.

She was also the type of teacher that you could talk to if you had a personal problem. Her patience and understanding was always appreciated during difficult times.

Form 2.7 VALUING LEARNING

A Student's View

If you didn't think a teacher was interested in teaching and valued learning, which of the following would make you think she or he valued learning? Make some suggestions of your own.
 1. Including in the lessons interesting things that were not in your textbooks or curriculum guides
 2. Including references to what you are learning to daily living
 3. Being excited about finding out something new or solving a problem
 4. Making thoughtful comments about your progress
 5. Encouraging you to learn something in which you are interested

6. Encouraging your interest in something new
7. Engaging in finding out more about things
8. Engaging in activities with students
9. Doing things expected of students such as painting, writing, reading, keeping up with current events
10. Knowing what is new in a subject area, for example, developments in science, research findings

---

MODELING AND COMMUNICATING ATTITUDES AND BEHAVIORS

The fifth principle of classroom management is communicating and modeling the first four:

> Effective classroom managers communicate and model respect, consistency, responsibility for learning, and valuing and enjoying learning, and they expect the same of their students.

The importance of respecting students, being consistent and credible and therefore dependable, assuming responsibility for learning, and valuing and enjoying learning have already been discussed. All of these behaviors can be powerful influences on students, but the essence of all teacher attributes that affect student behavior is modeling the behaviors expected of students.

A teacher with ten years of teaching experience wrote the following account of her first year teaching and her awakening to the effects of the model she exhibited to her students.

> As I fearfully walked down the hall toward the room that would become my stage for the next ten months, I thought about my audience, a group of 25 third graders from one of the toughest, poorest high crime areas of New York. I thought about the reaction of my friends when told that this is where I would be working, and the warnings from the principal to control the class, and not to allow the children to walk all over me. It was then that I decided what part I would play on that stage.
>
> That day, and for several years, I played the part of a teacher who hardly ever smiled, even when things were funny. One who was authoritarian and systematic to the point where students' interests, curiosity, and

feelings were inhibited. One who demanded respect without giving any, who would not tolerate "child's play" or develop social or emotional relationships with students. . . .

My students knew not to smile in class or make jokes that would make others laugh. They knew not to talk or ask questions unless I said they could. They knew I wasn't interested in their personal lives and, therefore, did not approach me with their problems. They knew I wasn't a friend, but a "Teacher." They knew to do what they were told without question—to walk down the hall like soldiers, and sit at their desk with folded hands. My principal commended this. My co-workers envied it. I felt proud.

I later came to realize that the behavior I modeled all those years was a result of three things. One, the preconceived idea I had about those children which led me to fear them and, consequently, to react in a way that would have them fear me instead. Two, my lack of awareness of the behaviors I was modeling and their effects on the students, and three, my ignorance of alternative methods for controlling the classroom.

Although the behavior I modeled was deliberate and planned, and my motivation to control the classroom legitimate, I failed to meet one of my primary responsibilities as an educator—which is to enhance the interests and social development of students. I was modeling behaviors that would produce undesirable learning effects, rather than positive and desirable ones. I should have been more encouraging and open to questions, since this can be a sign of interest in the topic and not one of defiance. I could have reinforced curiosity and interest by commenting on my own interests, showing a more human side of this person they saw only as "Teacher." I could have modeled the values, attitudes, and behaviors that I sought in the classroom, rather than just demand them. I could have showed them the reasoning behind my decisions so that they might later use that reasoning in other situations. This would have also helped them see me as a credible and reliable person that they could trust. I could have listened more and treated them more politely, fostering mutual respect, as well as giving them a sense of dignity and self-esteem. I could have shown more cooperation and flexibility, promoting a sense of unity among the group. I could have been a better model . . . a better teacher.

The effects of modeling can be equally powerful with older students. The following comments were made by college students.

The one thing that really impressed me about this course was the teacher. I found her to be quite honest and a pleasant leader to have. Her attitude toward students seemed one of complete respect. She practices what she preaches.

I like this course because the teacher practices what she teaches. Her candor is refreshing.

First and most important to me as a student was liking the teacher. I found this class both pleasant and personal. I believe I got out of this class what was intended.

The best thing about this course was the teacher. If a teacher has a pleasant personality and a sense of humor, they could be teaching anything and I would enjoy it. The teacher served as a good model for the kind of teacher I would like to be, and that is far more important than the accumulation of any factual data, which brings me to another positive aspect of this course. We were not asked to memorize anything that we could not apply in our teaching career. Another thing, she was consistent, never once did she shift ground on us, the tests were fair. She taught the objectives she originally told us from the very first day. I thoroughly enjoyed the class.

Modeling is a teaching tool that works even when we fail to plan for it to work. Students learn from modeling, whether it be deliberate or incidental; and its effects can be powerful. Social scientists tell us that much of what we know has been learned by imitating models rather than through formal systematic instruction. Children learn their native language by imitating. They become socialized into the family and other groups, even school, by observing models; and their attitudes and values are generally learned by example. Teachers who consciously use modeling as a method of instruction deliberately model a desired behavior and direct students to imitate the behavior. Problem-solving techniques, scientific methods of inquiry, reading with expression, and so on are modeled in many classrooms. However, much of what we learn through modeling is not consciously and deliberately planned; it is incidental or learned by chance.

Modeling effects are strongest in ambiguous situations where it is not clear what is expected or what to do. Students' uncertainty in unfamiliar situations forces them to look to models for guidance. Remember what your parents told you when you were nervous and anxiety ridden about how to behave at a fancy restaurant, a party, a dinner, or a reception? "If you don't know how to act, look for someone you think knows what to do and follow that person's lead." Modeling effects may be particularly strong at the beginning of a school year, when students do not know what to expect of teachers. They observe, "size up" their new model, form opinions and expectations, and act accordingly. It is important during the early days of the school year that the teacher's behavior conveys the climate she or he wants to create. The frequently given advice to preservice and beginning teachers, "Don't smile until Christmas," does not take into account the effects of modeling, unless of course, you want a nonsmiling classroom (Emmer, Evertson, and Anderson, 1980). (See Form 2.8.)

Form 2.8 DO AS I SAY, NOT AS I DO

1. My teacher interrupts me without a word of apology, but if I interrupt my teacher, he says I am rude.
2. My teacher is a grouch and mean but expects me to be pleasant and nice.
3. My teacher expects me to like school but has dull, boring, slow moving lessons.
4. My teacher tells me my work is poor but doesn't show me how to improve.
5. I can't read my teacher's handwriting, but he expects mine to be readable.
6. My teacher says he will allow me to do something special, but he never does.
7. My teacher says he will grade my homework, but I saw it in his trash can.
8. My teacher tells me to listen but never listens to me.
9. My teacher eats in the classroom, but I am not allowed.
10. My teacher says I can't talk in the cafeteria, but he does.

Students are inclined to imitate behaviors of teachers they like or admire, and behaviors that they perceive as effective, rewarding, relevant, and pertinent. Students are less prone to imitate behaviors of teachers they do not respect or like. On the other hand, when a teacher models undesirable behaviors such as ridicule, hostility, and sarcasm, students will often model those behaviors when they are in that teacher's classroom. Also, when a teacher rejects and "picks on" students, their peers may imitate this teacher and also "pick on" those students (Good and Brophy, 1987). Sadly, teachers are often unaware of how they model or fail to model appropriate behavior.

Both verbal and nonverbal language can effectively and precisely model the teacher's intent; it can also convey the "wrong" message. The teacher's verbal communication skills are crucial to effective instruction. Explaining things, choosing the right word, rephrasing, simplifying, and so on, are examples of verbal skills used in teaching. Choice of the word or phrase will determine the quality or even the correctness of the message. For example, teacher X makes plans to increase students' participation in the classroom. Instead of calling on one student to answer a question, teacher X reads a math problem and says, "Thumbs up if we add, thumbs down if we subtract." When the thumbs are pointed, teacher X asks, "Who is right?" "Who is wrong?" A better question is "What is wrong?" One question says the person is wrong; the other says the answer is wrong—a big difference. We need to choose our words carefully and efficiently with a conscious knowledge of effects. Words can and do hurt students.

Nonverbal communication can be just as powerful as the spoken word and some nonverbal behaviors can be just as carefully modeled and chosen as words. We consciously touch others, smile, frown, stand straight, or slouch; however, unlike verbal communication, which we choose, many of our nonverbal responses are beyond our control, for example, blushing, crying, showing anger, surprise, and fear. These automatic responses often reveal whether our verbal responses are genuine or phony and model true feelings, beliefs, and intentions.

Educators, psychologists, and researchers have long recognized the power of nonverbal communication. The classic story of Clever Hans is an example of the power and subtleties of nonverbal communication. Clever Hans was a horse owned by a German mathematics professor. The professor taught Hans to solve difficult math problems and tap his foot to indicate the answers. Animal experts and scientists who investigated the horse's behavior agreed that the animal could indeed solve problems presented to him and that no one cued Hans on when to tap his foot. However, in 1911, Oskar Pfungst (1965) was able to identify the source of Hans's cleverness. He proved that the person who asked Hans a question had to know the answer and that Hans had to see the questioner. He showed that a slight forward movement of the questioner's head was the horse's cue to start tapping, and a slight upward head movement or a raised eyebrow was the cue to stop. Even more surprising, he demonstrated that the questioner was unaware that he was cuing. It seems that our every stance, hand movement, or raised eyebrow can and does cue students just as effectively as Hans. The question for teachers then is "What am I communicating?" We should not be surprised by the answer; we should strive to model purposefully and conscientiously, both verbally and nonverbally, the messages we intend and the behavior we expect of students.

SUMMARY

At least five teacher attributes are essential to effective classroom management. Effective managers

1. must respect and have the respect of students,
2. are consistent and therefore credible and dependable,

3. assume responsibility for students' learning,
4. value and enjoy learning, and
5. communicate and model the above and expect the same from students.

When you, the teacher, respect your students and they know that you do, they in turn tend to respect you. When you are consistent, your students will find you credible and dependable; they will believe you and rely on you. You, in turn, will find them credible and dependable. When you assume responsibility for learning in your classroom, your students tend to assume some responsibility for their own learning. When you value and enjoy learning and students know it, they rise to the challenge and tend to do the same. When you have communicated and modeled these attributes in your interactions with students, you have created an atmosphere in which most students will accept your management and discipline procedures.

Students of all ages cry out for teachers who are human and humane. They seek out adults who listen to them and respect their ideas. They reach for teachers who are not "God," a computer or an "untouchable." Most students want a teacher who will not be afraid of them and not be afraid to be themselves—a model.

Even when teachers have acquired these powerful attributes, as previously noted there is no such thing as a perfect teacher and perfect students in a perfectly managed classroom. So there is still a need for preventing and resolving discipline and management problems. Chapters 3 and 4 are devoted to preventing management and discipline problems.

QUESTIONS AND ACTIVITIES

2.1 Respect is manifested in a myriad of ways. Define respect in your own words.

2.2 Why is trust such an important part of respect?

2.3 Why is respect important to ego strength?

2.4 Why is respect of teachers for students necessary for successful classroom management?

2.5 Which of the teacher behaviors in Form 2.1 are appropriate for working with elementary students? Secondary students? Both?

2.6 List at least five things you can do to help you demonstrate respect for others.

2.7 Choose a behavior that shows your respect for students. Plan a strategy to practice that behavior. Your strategy should include practice, conditions, time, place, and so on.

2.8 List some factors that affect communication between teachers and students.

2.9 Make a list of attitudes and then convey those attitudes in a nonverbal way to your peers.

2.10 Write a description of a teacher you admire.

2.11 Practice modeling a specified behavior in a simulated or "real" classroom.

2.12 Make a list of reasons why consistent teacher behavior is so important.

2.13 Set an objective to change one of your behaviors and develop a long- and short-range plan.

2.14 Do you really value learning? Tell how you show that you do.

2.15 Choose a behavior you think you almost always model. Ask your friends to verify your view.

2.16 Make a list of the ways you show enthusiasm.

2.17 List behaviors of overly restrictive and overly permissive teachers.

REFERENCES

Brophy, J., and Putnam, J. (1978). *Classroom Management in the Elementary Grades.* (Research Series 32). East Lansing, Mich.: Michigan State University, Institute for Research on Teaching.

Brophy, J., and Rohrkemper, M. (1981). "The Influence of Problem-Ownership on Teacher Perceptions of Strategies for Coping with Problem Students." *Journal of Educational Psychology,* 73, pp. 295–311.

Collins, M. L. (1976). "The Effects of Training for Enthusiasm on the Enthusiasm Displayed by Preservice Elementary Teachers." Doctoral dissertation. Syracuse, N.Y.: Syracuse University. Quoted in *Practical Applications of Research* (1981). Newsletter of Phi Delta Kappa's Center on Evaluation, Development and Research, p. 3, p. 4. Bloomington, Ind.

Crow, M., and Bonney, M. (1975). "Recognizing the Authoritarian Personality Syndrome in Educators." *Phi Delta Kappan,* 57(1), pp. 40–44.

Emmer, E., Evertson, C., and Anderson, L. (1980). "Effective Classroom Management at the Beginning of the School Year." *Elementary School Journal,* 80, pp. 219–231.

Good, T., Biddle, B., and Brophy, J. (1975). *Teachers Make a Difference.* New York: Holt, Rinehart, and Winston.

Good, T., and Brophy, J. (1987). *Looking in Classrooms* (4th ed.). New York: Harper and Row, p. 228, pp. 190–191, 174–179.

Good, T., and Brophy, J. (1986). "School Effects." In M. Wittrock (ed.) *Handbook of Research on Teaching* (3rd ed.). New York: Macmillan.

Gordon, T. (1974). *T.E.T.: Teacher Effectiveness Training.* New York: Peter H. Wyden.

Jones, F. (1979, June). "The Gentle Art of Classroom Discipline." *National Elementary Principal*, 58, pp. 26–32.

Kohn, A. (1990). "The ABC's of Caring." *Teacher, 1*(4), pp. 52–58.

Kounin, J. (1970). *Discipline and Group Management in Classrooms.* New York: Holt, Rinehart, and Winston.

Maslow, A. (1968). *Toward a Psychology of Being.* New York: Van Nostrand.

Norman, J., and Harris, M. (1981). *The Private Life of the American Teenager.* New York: Rawson, Wade.

Pfungst, O. (1965). *Clever Hans. The Horse of Mr. Von Osten.* Translated by C. L. Rahn. New York: Holt, Rinehart, and Winston.

Pickhardt, C. (1978, November). "Fear in the Schools: How Students Make Teachers Feel Afraid." *Educational Leadership, 36*(3), pp. 107–112.

Redl, F. (1966). *When We Deal with Children.* New York: The Free Press, p. 303.

Rosenshine, B., and Furst, N. (1970). "Enthusiastic Teaching: A Research Review." *School Review*, 78(4), pp. 449–514.

Sizer, T. (1984). *Horace's Compromise.* Boston: Houghton Mifflin.

PART
Two

PREVENTING MANAGEMENT PROBLEMS

*I*n Part One of this text we have found that in order to manage a classroom effectively, teachers must (1) respect students and earn students' respect, (2) behave consistently and be perceived by students as credible and dependable, (3) assume responsibility for students' learning, (4) value and enjoy learning and expect the same from students, and (5) model these behaviors in the classroom.

These attributes are necessary for successful management and discipline, but they are not sufficient—in other words, "being nice" is not enough. Too often the preeminent concerns of students are socializing, finding security, getting attention, and building self-worth, not studying and learning. Teachers may possess essential personal attributes and insist students be quiet, attentive, cooperative, and interested, but at the same time students continue to pursue basic needs for identity and maturity. No matter how respectful, consistent, enthusiastic, and conscientious the teacher, some students will test the teacher's authority; therefore, teachers who would be effective managers must do more than model desirable attitudes.

Recent investigations by numerous researchers (Kounin, 1970; Brophy and Good, 1986; Doyle, 1986) indicate that one significant difference between effective and ineffective classroom managers is that effective managers demonstrate more behaviors that *prevent* inappropriate student behavior. They recognize that the key to successful management is prevention, and they plan to prevent problems before they happen.

Part Two of this book is devoted to two areas of teacher behavior that research findings indicate contribute to preventing misconduct. These two areas are (1) planning for managing classrooms, and (2) maximizing student attention to learning.

Chapter 3 identifies aspects of classroom management and discipline that require careful organization and planning, gives examples of planning for preventing problems, and suggests methods for implementing those plans.

Chapter 4 identifies and describes teacher behaviors and teaching techniques that maximize student attention to learning and prevent management and discipline problems.

When you have completed Part Two you should be able to prevent many management and discipline problems through planning for managing classrooms and maximizing students' attention to learning.

Chapter
3

Planning for Managing Classrooms

INTRODUCTION AND OBJECTIVES

When teachers plan for instruction, they plan to achieve both long- and short-range goals. As you know, it may take weeks, months, or even years to accomplish long-range objectives. Short-range goals, achieved daily and step by step, bring the long-range vision to fruition. Long- and short-range goals are developed for a class as a whole and for individual students or groups who may need remediation or challenges.

Just as teachers plan long-range and short-range instructional goals for the group and for individuals, those who are effective managers plan for managing classrooms. They envision the kind of classroom climate they want to develop, and they set long-range and short-range goals for the group and individual students in order to achieve that vision. Too often teachers simply hope the class will be "good." We dream of a classroom where all students listen, follow directions, and enjoy learning, but we have few plans; if any, to achieve this grand order of listening, learning, and obeying (Evertson and Emmer, 1982a).

Effective managers realize that one can know exactly and precisely the content to be taught but that one can never know or predict precisely how students will behave. Therefore, teachers who envision themselves as leaders of classrooms where students behave appro-

priately but sometimes unpredictably plan for the prevention of behavior and management problems, which can be found in varying
degrees in all classrooms.

Effective classroom managers *plan* to prevent management problems and
teach discipline.

After you have completed Chapter 3 you will (1) recognize the
importance of planning for management and discipline, (2) be able to
plan for managing a classroom, and (3) be able to utilize techniques
suggested in this text for preventing problems.
Specifically, preservice and beginning teachers will:

- develop and use seating patterns to prevent management and
  discipline problems;
- plan for efficient use of materials;
- formulate a set of appropriate and clearly stated rules and
  procedures;
- develop plans for teaching rules and procedures;
- communicate rules, directions, expectations, and consequences
  of actions systematically and efficiently;
- utilize all available sources of information to "know" students;
- acquire and utilize with-it-ness;
- list and describe aspects of classroom management that can be
  planned; and
- plan for prevention of individual and group behavior problems.

ORGANIZING THE CLASSROOM

Getting off to a good start is essential to establishing the kind of classroom you envision. The classroom atmosphere that evolves during the
first days and early weeks of school will affect the climate throughout
the year. Effective managers know that the key to successful management is preventing problems, and they recognize that success in preventing problems comes from careful and systematic planning. Before
students arrive the very first day, they have already planned a good

beginning (Emmer, Evertson, and Anderson, 1980). One of the first things effective managers do prior to the opening of school is plan their room arrangements and efficient use of materials.

Effective classroom managers organize their room and teaching materials.

Everything in a classroom affects the environment. Some settings stimulate students to do their best; other settings seduce students to "fool around" and to ignore their tasks. Teachers who have a vision of an effectively managed classroom, populated by students who are well disciplined, make plans to develop a setting designed to achieve those goals.

One powerful but often overlooked and under-estimated influence on classroom climate is the seating arrangement. Students' chairs and desks should be arranged so that both the teacher and students can move about easily. The teacher should be able to see the faces of all students; students should be able to see the teacher, chalkboards, maps, screens, and other instructional materials without straining or moving their seats. One seating configuration that meets these criteria is the traditional "rows of seats" with walking space between each row and each seat.

A seating pattern commonly seen in elementary classrooms is students' desks grouped in twos, fours, or even sixes. This makes it impossible for all students to face the teacher at any one time. This configuration might be useful for small groups working together; however, whole-group instruction cries out for face-to-face interaction. Students who are seated with their backs to the teacher soon learn they can be inattentive and disruptive and the teacher cannot see them. Not all classrooms are large enough to allow teachers the freedom to arrange desks ideally. In such cases you should experiment with various arrangements and choose the one that allows you to achieve your instructional, management and discipline goals.

A careful analysis of traffic patterns, closets, equipment, and supplies in a classroom can help the teacher anticipate possible problems. For example, when a pencil sharpener is surrounded by students' desks, some may spend more time trimming pencils and watching others trim pencils than when desks are placed as far away as possible from this distraction. Other distractions are pet cages, water fountains, supply closets, show-and-tell materials, and so on.

In addition to seating arrangements, effective managers plan for storage and accessibility of books and other materials. In the early grades paper, pencils, and art materials are often supplied by the school district. These supplies should be placed in an area where there is little traffic and congestion and where they can be easily reached. If materials such as textbooks and workbooks will be used, make sure there is a copy for every student. Your planning should include the development and duplication of bibliographies, course requirements, and whatever is needed to begin instruction immediately and effectively on the very first day of school. You should also prepare the room for students by developing bulletin board displays, pictures, and objects intended to attract student interest. The appearance of your room will determine students' perceptions of you and the classroom climate you want to develop. It communicates order or disorder, enthusiasm or boredom, interest or detachment. In fact, it communicates your view of the nature of teaching and the teacher's role as well as your perception of students and their role.

Teachers must plan and establish the classroom climate just as they plan curriculum and teaching strategies in the academic disciplines. Effective managers in both elementary and secondary schools visualize the kind of classroom climate they want and set both long- and short-range goals to achieve their vision. They plan seating arrangements and procedures for using materials that will best contribute to that vision. Effective managers know that planning for a good beginning eliminates surprises; they try to leave nothing to happenstance.

ESTABLISHING RULES AND PROCEDURES

Any group of people, including, and perhaps especially, students in classrooms, need rules to live by and procedure for carrying them out. Rules give us standards for a broad group or cluster of behaviors. Procedures give us the details and interpretations that tell us how to act out the rules. Classroom rules are needed in order to accomplish the business of teaching and learning and the nurturing of students' self-worth. Effective classroom managers anticipate and recognize the need for the regulation of student behavior, and they develop and teach rules and procedures that specify what is appropriate.

> Effective classroom managers establish rules and procedures prior to or at the beginning of school.

The responsibility for establishing classroom rules ultimately lies with the teacher. Some teachers involve students in rule making, others develop rules independently. Most teachers establish at least some of the rules themselves, and effective managers do so prior to the beginning of the school year.

The genesis of rules is the vision the teacher has of the kind of classroom he or she wants to create. You are already aware that teachers have different beliefs about child development, what constitutes an ideal classroom environment, and how teachers should interact with students. The rules established will reflect diversity in teachers' thinking and in the need for rules. The behavior standards of elementary teachers may differ from those of secondary teachers; standards in inner-city schools may differ from those in affluent suburbs; and standards in science laboratories may differ from those in art classes. The rules in Forms 3.1, 3.2, 3.3, 3.4, and 3.5 were developed and used by teachers. They are not given as examples of perfect rules, but as illustrations of a variety of expectations teachers have of students. Regardless of the teacher's view of child development, the kind of classroom climate the teacher envisions, the subject, or the age and socioeconomic status of students, rules are needed to regulate common categories of behavior, such as working conditions, using materials and facilities, listening, and general group living.

Form 3.1 RULES FOR A THIRD GRADE CLASSROOM

The following rules set the standards for behavior in a third grade classroom. What do you think of this set of rules? Can you make them better? Has any area of conduct been omitted?

1. Homework is to be done always.
2. While the teacher is with a group, no one is to disturb her except in case of emergency.
3. Stay in your seats quietly during seatwork.

4. Students are to walk on their way to class and within the classroom.
5. During class time silence is to be kept in the hallways.

Form 3.2 RULES FOR A SEVENTH GRADE SOCIAL STUDIES CLASS

Rules

1. Be in seat, ready to work when bell rings.
2. Raise hand and wait to be called on before talking.
3. Always be prepared.
4. Keep hands, feet, and objects to yourself.
5. Eating, drinking, and chewing gum are forbidden.

Consequences

1. Name on board
2. Name on board and one check: WARNING
3. Name on board and two checks: 20-MINUTE DETENTION
4. Name on board and three checks: CALL HOME AND SEND TO COUNSELOR
5. Name on board and four checks: VISIT TO ADMINISTRATION

Rewards

1. Star by name on display chart (weekly)
2. Pass on homework
3. Gets pencil after four perfect weeks
4. Gets certificate after nine weeks

Form 3.3 RULES FOR A JUNIOR HIGH SCHOOL CLASSROOM

Dear Parent(s):

I will be your child's _____ teacher this school year (19____). In order to guarantee the optimum educational climate for your son or daughter, I have developed the following Classroom Guidelines, which will be in effect at *all* times.

Students must comply with the following rules:
1. Follow directions the first time they are given.
2. Be in seat, ready to work when the bell rings.
3. Always bring to class textbook(s), notebook, and something to write with.
4. Keep hands, feet, objects, and personal comments to yourself.
5. During lectures or instruction of any kind, if a student would like to ask a question, he or she must raise hand.

First time student breaks a rule: WARNING
Second time student breaks a rule: ONE DETENTION

Third time student breaks a rule: TWO (2) DETENTIONS
Fourth time student breaks a rule: TWO (2) DETENTIONS AND CALL PARENT(S)
Fifth time student breaks a rule: TWO (2) DETENTIONS, CALL PARENT(S), SEND STUDENT TO PRINCIPAL
  If a student is severely disruptive, he/she will be sent immediately to the principal!
  It should be noted that although not listed in the Classroom Guidelines, students will from time to time be rewarded with free class time, no-homework nights, special class activities, and so on, for cooperation with the Guidelines.
  In order for this plan to have its greatest effect, I need your support. Please discuss this letter with your child, sign it and return it to me. Thank you for your cooperation.

Form 3.4 SENIOR HIGH SCHOOL CLASSROOM PROCEDURES

Welcome to _____Senior High.
  For your safety and in order to promote the best climate for learning, the following rules have been made known to you and explained completely:
  1. Remain in your seat during the entire period.
  2. Raise your hand in order to be recognized or to be excused.
  3. Keep your hands, feet, and objects to yourself.
  4. Follow directions the first time they are given.
The consequences of not following these rules are:
  1. First time: WARNING
  2. Second time: DAILY CONDUCT GRADE OF E
  3. Third time: CALL TO PARENTS
  4. Fourth time: ADMINISTRATION CONFERENCE

Form 3.5 ART CLASSES STUDIO RULES

  1. Store personal items in place indicated before class starts.
  2. Students must be seated and quiet for roll call.
  3. Each student is responsible for getting out his or her materials.
  4. Students are expected to work on their projects 40–45 minutes each class period.
  5. Talking must be kept at a reasonable noise level.
  6. Students must have an official pass to leave the room.
  7. All school policies must be adhered to in the studio.
  8. Each student is required to clean his or her own work area during clean-up time.

The purpose of rules is to make teaching and learning possible in a physically and psychologically safe environment. Rules should facilitate effective and efficient classroom management. When appropriate rules are accepted by students and enforced consistently, routine procedural activities and group living can take care of themselves and free the teacher to instruct and the students to learn.

It goes without saying that we should avoid developing a set of inappropriate rules. Inappropriate rules are useless—perhaps disastrous—because poorly chosen rules will create serious management and discipline problems. A good way to test a rule is to ask, "Is it reasonable for students to meet this expectation?" For example, is the following rule reasonable? "There will be absolute silence and absolutely no moving about the room without the teacher's permission." You can readily see this requires the teacher to decide continually who can get out of a seat and who can talk and then grant that permission. In a classroom with 30 students who need to use restrooms, get materials, and seek help, the teacher will be inundated with requests and will spend an inordinate amount of time simply enforcing this one rule. This rule may not only be difficult to enforce, but may also be unreasonable in relation to the students' developmental levels. Rules are not reasonable if they do not take into account how long students can listen, work independently, give attention, or understand the consequences of obedience and disobedience.

You may already be familiar with the stages of students' cognitive development identified by Jean Piaget and others. Certainly these developmental stages must be taken into account when rules, rewards, and consequences are developed. In addition to the identification of cognitive stages, Piaget, Lawrence Kohlberg, and others have identified developmental stages of moral judgment, and they have suggested behaviors characteristic of each stage (Piaget, 1932; Kohlberg and Turiel, 1971). Teachers need to understand as much as possible the development of moral judgment and to realize that the various stages will determine students' views of rules, rewards, and punishments. This knowledge helps ascertain if rules are reasonable.

The four stages of moral development identified by Piaget explain in some measure students' acceptance or rejection of authority. In stage 1, up to age 3, he found that children do not obey rules because they are rules; they merely imitate obedience. In other words, they copy the behavior of the adult who models adherence to the rule. In stage 2, ages 3 or 4 to 6, children know and can state the rules, but they change the rules to accommodate their behavior. For example, if the rules say a child may have three tries at guessing where something is hidden and the child does not guess correctly, she or he will continue to guess—thereby changing the rule to guessing until the correct hiding place is named. In stage 3, ages 7 or 8 to 11 or 12, students accept rules as absolute law and rigidly adhere to them. During this stage students are sometimes described as having an exaggerated sense of fairness. They will demand that rules be enforced to the letter of the law by the authority figure. In stage 4, beyond age 12, students understand why rules are necessary, and the morality of cooperation becomes important. At this stage students seek group membership and peer approval.

Piaget also studied the child's view of blame or culpability and found that young children see blame determined by the behavior, not by the intention. In this view a child who accidentally tears five pages in a book would be guiltier than a child who deliberately tears one page. As their sense of moral judgment develops, after age 10, students take intentionality into account.

Kohlberg and Turiel have also identified stages of development that affect students' perception of rules. At Level I, the premoral stage, children do not reason about right and wrong. Instead, "right" is seen as behavior that is rewarded and "wrong" as behavior that is punished. Morality is seen in terms of consequences. At Level II, morality of conventional role conformity, the child conforms to rules in order to win and keep the approval of others, such as parents, peers, teachers, or other authority figures. Behavior is "right" if others seem to approve and "like me" when I behave this way. It is "wrong" when others disapprove. At Level III, the morality of self-accepted principles, the students' own view of right and wrong begins to emerge and take precedence; children begin to recognize morality in rules and contracts. Because formal, operational, cognitive thinking is required in Level III, it appears that most elementary school students function at Levels I and II. They perceive right and wrong to be determined by rewards and punishment, and they conform in order to be accepted. Most students are probably not able to reason abstractly and ideally about the morality of specific laws, rules, and behaviors until the high school and adult years, if then. Remember that just as there will be students in your classroom at different stages of cognitive development, you will also have students at various stages of moral development and judgment. When rules are established and enforced, these differences should not be forgotten.

Moral development theories indicate that students in the lower grades accept adult authority to a greater degree than do older students. Therefore, teachers of lower grades may have less difficulty enforcing rules than teachers in the secondary school. Students in the intermediate grades will expect teachers to "be fair" and enforce rules without consideration of intentions. Junior and senior high school students will have a sense of group cooperation and peer approval, which teachers need to take into account. Teachers who work with older students probably should involve them in determining and establishing rules that are necessary and reasonable.

In addition to being appropriate, rules must also be simple and clear, written, and flexible. Some argue against written rules on the premise that "you can't write everything" and that students think they can get away with behaviors that aren't specifically forbidden. Written rules, however, are more likely than oral rules to be stated carefully, objectively and thoughtfully. In addition, written rules are more likely to be known and understood by students and consistently enforced by teachers. For instance, oral rules may be communicated when some students are absent, some students don't hear or understand, and sometimes the rule exists only in the teacher's head.

Rules should be posted somewhere in the classroom. Some secondary teachers and art, music, and other special teachers may not have classrooms of their own. In this case it is a good policy to make copies of the rules and give them to each student. Giving students their own copy of class rules may be a good policy even when you have your own classroom with the rules posted. You may also want to send a copy to parents and guardians. Written rules eliminate students' excuses for not knowing the rules and can be easily referred to when infractions occur or when conferencing with parents.

The form in which a rule is stated may influence its effectiveness. Effective classroom managers devise five to eight general rules that apply to a wide spectrum of student behaviors, such as, "Treat others with respect," and then identify specific behaviors, actions, or procedures that clarify the general behavior. For example, General Rule: Treat others with respect.

Specific observable behaviors that show respect:

- Ask permission before you use others' property.
- Share materials.
- Wait until others finish talking before you speak.
- Take your turn in class activities.
- Keep your hands and feet to yourself.

Rules must also be stated clearly and simply in language that is easily understood. Both general and specific rules should state concisely and, if possible, in a positive mode what is expected of students. Notice the difference in the following rule statements:

1. Students should remember to listen to classmates, the teacher, guest speakers, the principal, or others who are talking.
2. Listen when others are talking.

The first sentence is too wordy. A short, concise statement is more easily remembered.

1. Don't run in the halls.
2. Walk in the halls.

The second rule is stated positively; the first is a negative statement. Undesirable behavior may sometimes be suggested by stating rules in a negative manner. When rules are positive, you utilize the power of suggestion in a positive way.

A final criterion for writing rules is flexibility. Hard and fast rules can create more problems than they solve. Some room for interpretation is generally needed. You can readily see problems that can arise with rules such as:

1. Assignments are never accepted late.
2. You must always get permission to move from your seat.
3. There must be absolutely no talking during lunch.

See Form 3.6 for rules that may cause more problems than they solve.

Form 3.6 ARCHIE BUNKER'S UNENFORCEABLE AND INAPPROPRIATE RULES AND PROCEDURES

Tardiness	Tardiness for any reason is not tolerated. No one may keep you out of class unless I previously have given my approval. You will suffer the consequences. Do not bother me with excuses, and *none* will be accepted.
Class Cut	Any time you cut class your name will be turned in to the assistant principal. You may not make up any work and you will receive bad grades.
Appearance	If you are unsure as to what the proper attire is after checking with the school rules, *don't ask me!* Just don't wear the outfit.
Attitude	All of the following must be strictly adhered to, or you will be immediately removed from the rest of the class. a. Do not eat, drink, or chew anything in class. b. Do not use inappropriate language. c. Do not make unsolicited comments.

d.   Do not speak if anyone else is speaking.

e.   Do not show disrespect to me at any time or in any way.

f.   Never offer excuses for yourself.

Academic   If you do not bring your materials to class every day, you will be segregated from the rest of the students, and you will not be able to complete any of the day's work. Also, you will receive zeros and will never be able to make up work.

The grading scale is as follows:

A = 94 to 100

B = 85 to 93

C = 75 to 84

D = 65 to 74

F = 0 to 64

If you have D average, I may override your grade and give you an F, especially if you have been a negative influence in this class.

Conduct Cuts   Any time you misbehave, I will give you a conduct cut. When you have accumulated enough, your grade will be dropped.

Passes   You cannot leave the classroom during class sessions, except in case of an emergency.

After you have established a few general rules that set standards for classroom behavior, you should communicate to students the procedures you want. Procedures such as turning in homework, providing headings on papers, beginning a period of instruction, changing groups or classes, sharpening pencils, completing assignments, turning in incomplete work, making up missed assignments or tests, grading, changing papers, and so on, should be communicated to students. At secondary school levels, where assignments often require work more than overnight work, written procedures are a good idea. At all grade levels, posting assignments reminds students of their responsibilities.

We have already said that the need for rules and procedures can be anticipated even before school begins. Situations arise, however, that cannot be foreseen by the teachers. When these occur, analyze the problem, look for the source, and try to identify specific behaviors creating the problem. These behaviors can then serve as the basis for establishing rules and procedures to overcome the problem. For example, a common problem—often unforeseen, especially by beginning teachers—is efficient and safe procedures for using restrooms. Students sometimes perceive restrooms as hideouts where they can dawdle or socialize. Teachers must always be cognizant of potentially serious problems that can arise with older students. They must be especially alert to smoking, drug use, and sexual behavior. The hazards of hard and fast rules can also cause problems for young children.

Restroom use can run smoothly, or, it can be a consistently recurring management problem. Many teachers are amazingly creative in devising procedures for using restrooms. For example, a common classroom rule is, "The restrooms are to be used by one person at a time." In order to enforce this rule, one second grade teacher cut two large keys from tag board. She colored one key blue and labeled it BOYS, one key pink and labeled it GIRLS. The keys were laminated, placed on a string, and hung on the wall near the exit to the bathroom. When a student wanted to use the restroom all he or she had to do was see if the "key" was available. No interruption of the teacher was necessary. Of course, the procedure for taking and returning the key to its proper place had to be learned and practiced until it became routine. The same teacher also had hung on her desk three more keys of neutral colors labeled with the teacher's name and room number. These keys were used for hall, office, and library passes. The whole procedure worked beautifully, but only because it had been practiced, mastered, and enforced.

Thus far in this chapter you have learned that, prior to or at the beginning of school, effective classroom managers plan their room arrangements and methods of handling materials. Specifically, you have found that room arrangements should make it possible for

1. the teacher to see all students from any place in the room,
2. the teacher to walk around and between students' seats,
3. all students to see the teacher,
4. normal routines to proceed without constant help from the teacher, and
5. books and supplies to be easily accessed.

You have also learned some rules for developing and writing appropriate rules. These are:

1. The rule should be needed.
2. The rule should be reasonable.
3. The rule should take into account the cognitive and moral development levels of students.
4. The rule should be simple and clear.
5. The rule should be flexible.
6. If possible, the rule should be stated in a positive mode.
7. Perhaps the rule should be written.

Some procedures for using rules have also been suggested:

1. Formulate rules prior to or at the beginning of school.
2. Post rules.
3. Give students copies of rules.
4. Have a minimum number of rules.
5. Establish consequences.
6. Teach the rules.

TEACHING RULES AND PROCEDURES

It has already been stated that the purpose for establishing rules and procedures is to facilitate teaching and learning in a physically and psychologically safe environment. For this purpose to be achieved, rules and procedures must be appropriate and must also be followed so consistently and thoroughly that they become routine. Routines that are followed without reminders, reprimands, punishments, and other impediments facilitate the entire management process and leave more time for teachers to teach and students to learn. Remember that appropriate behavior by students does not automatically happen simply because you have formulated a "perfect" set of rules and procedures.

Effective classroom managers teach rules and procedures.

Once you have thoughtfully and carefully developed appropriate standards of behavior, you need to plan the most effective method for teaching, implementing, and enforcing those standards. Rules alone do not affect classroom behavior. If rules are effective, students must know the rules, accept the rules, understand that they can be changed, and know what will happen when rules are broken. In order for these conditions to be met, research findings not only indicate that rules should be established but also that they should be systematically taught during the first days of the school year (Emmer, Evertson, and Anderson, 1980).

"Systematically taught" does not mean a spur-of-the-moment or incidental explanation. It means coherent, methodical planning and teaching. Just as teachers plan and teach knowledge and skills in a subject area, teachers who would have the kind of ideal classroom environment they envision also plan and teach their classroom rules and procedures.

The first step in teaching classroom rules is to present the rule to the class. Remember, general rules are often broad and may cover a large number of behaviors. If this is the case, you will need to present the rule as a long-range goal, and the specific observable behaviors may be presented as short-range objectives. Students in the upper elementary grades and junior and senior high school might be introduced to the general rule and a number of specific behaviors; young children might be presented the general rule and a smaller number of specific behaviors. Secondary students will already know many of the desired behaviors and will not need as much help in rule clarification.

Whatever the students' age level, be certain students clearly understand the meaning of a rule. Teachers sometimes assume that if students can read a rule, they also understand it. Differences in age, knowledge of vocabulary, and cultural background can all influence understanding and interpretation. For example, some children come from home backgrounds where cursing is defined as "using the Lord's name in vain." Hence any casual reference to God is cursing, but it may be alright to say "damn" if God's name is not used. Other children have been taught that "damn," "hell," and "darn" are curse words. Misunderstandings about whispering can also be quite common. Students may perceive whispering as low, soft-spoken, voiced speech. Demonstrating and modeling meaning can help ensure understanding and clarity of rule interpretation. To determine if students understand the rule, you may have them define in their own words key words or phrases or have them give examples of behaviors the rule indicates and those it does not.

Students must not only understand the rule, but also they must remember the rule. You may have the students write the rule or tell the rule to another student or to the entire class. If rules are essential for safety in laboratories, workshops, or playgrounds, you may want to test students on their knowledge of rules and require a minimum passing score before students are allowed in specified areas.

Once the rule has been presented and students know the rule and understand what it means, the next step is discussing reasons for the rule. Students need to know why the rule is necessary. When they agree and accept the fact that it is necessary, they are more likely to comply with the behaviors specified. Sometimes the necessity for rules may be taught simultaneously with reasons for remembering the rule. You should not only talk about the importance and necessity of each classroom rule, but you will also need to demonstrate what happens when the rule is obeyed and when it is ignored. Role playing situations with and without rules can graphically illustrate the disorderly and potentially dangerous situations that can result without rules. (See Form 3.7.)

Form 3.7 HELPING STUDENTS KNOW WHEN A RULE IS NEEDED

---

1. Put some instructional supplies on a table at the front of the room—scissors, paper, glue, books, and so on.
2. Have one student come to the table and get an object. Have other students observe.
3. Have five students get an object. Have other students observe.
4. Repeat step 3 with 20 students.
5. Have students discuss what they observed. Compare what was observed with 1 student, 5 students, 20 students.
6. Have students write a rule for getting supplies.

Effective classroom managers generally have students practice behaviors that are specified by rules. Differences in age and cultural background should be taken into account when you determine if practicing the rule is necessary. Older students certainly will not need to practice opening their textbooks quickly and efficiently; however, practicing simple behaviors may help young children remember the rules and increase compliance. One reason rules are posted is to help students remember them without constant reminders by the teacher. Rules should be posted in a highly visible part of the classroom, and those that pertain to a particular activity or workplace should be posted where the activity takes place or in that workplace. Rules that apply to using supplies should be placed where supplies are stored; rules for using the restroom should be placed near the restroom.

At this point in your study of effective management and discipline, you should have a vision of the ideal classroom climate you want to develop. This conception or vision may be in your head—an unwritten model. Try to write this vision down. You should also have a few simple rules that you believe are essential for the achievement of your ideal classroom as well as a list of procedures that will facilitate your management and discipline goals. Put your rules and procedures in writing. Evaluate them using the criteria given in this chapter. Choose one of your rules and an age and grade level, and use the following plan for teaching rules as a guide to develop a plan of your own. Remember, a lesson plan must have objectives, procedures, and a method of determining the effectiveness of the lesson.

A PLAN FOR TEACHING A RULE

Rule If you must leave your seat for any reason, move quietly around the room.

This rule may be appropriate for all ages, but the degree of emphasis will vary according to the age and needs of students. For example, 6-year-olds may have different reasons for leaving seats than do 15-year-olds. Laboratory settings may require leaving seats more than a lecture classroom.

Objectives Students will demonstrate knowledge, understanding, and compliance by leaving seats noiselessly, walking quietly, refraining from talking with other students, accomplishing goals for leaving seats, and returning to seats in the same manner. Few students, if any, will take notice when another student leaves his or her seat.

Procedures

1. To present the rule, state the rule and clarify terms. Ask, "What is moving quietly around the room?" Give and use examples. List and discuss reasons why students may need to leave their seats. Accept reasons that are valid, reject those that are not. A valid reason might be going to the restroom. An invalid reason might be to speak to another student about a party.
2. Discuss the reason for the rule, ask students for reasons. Include as many valid reasons as possible, but don't use a flimsy rationale. This makes the rule look ridiculous. Some questions for discussion might be: What would happen if everyone left their seats in an inappropriate manner? Why do we need to be quiet? Why are we in school? How does quiet behavior help us? Why do we need to be able to leave our seats quietly?
3. Give examples and test the rule: Try role playing with one student getting out of his or her seat and returning in an inappropriate manner. Try role playing with five students, and then

with the entire class. Try having one student practice leaving and returning to his or her seat in an appropriate manner. Try five students. Try all students. Discuss what happened. Have students draw conclusions about the procedures.

4. Establish consequences for breaking the rule: There must be a consequence for noncompliance and a reward for compliance depending on age, classroom climate, and so on. With some groups you may want to solicit suggestions. You, however, must have appropriate suggestions and make the final decision. Some consequences might be the loss of some special privilege or loss of points if you have a reward system. Rewards might be extra points or special privileges.

Evaluation Determine whether the number of students who fail to follow the rule diminishes. If problems develop relative to one or more reasons for leaving seats, reevaluate those reasons and change them if necessary. Remember, rules should be flexible.

CREATING A CLASSROOM CLIMATE THAT ENCOURAGES COMPLIANCE WITH RULES AND PROCEDURES

Appropriate and perfectly stated rules and procedures given to students and parents in written form, posted, and carefully taught during the first days of the school year do not guarantee a well-managed classroom. Somehow the teacher must see to it that the rules and procedures are followed and that students develop the self-discipline to comply, ideally without coercion. In classrooms of effective teachers and managers, students follow rules and procedures with little overt guidance or coaxing. Why do most students in these classrooms willingly live by the rules? Of course there is no one simple answer, but you have already learned in Chapter 2 that successful managers respect students; assume some responsibility for their learning; value and enjoy learning; are consistent, credible, and dependable; and model the same. These essential attitudes will be affected by what we know or do not know about the students we teach. In the cognitive area we all recognize the need to know students' ability and achievement levels in order to plan and instruct appropriately. Certainly it is just as necessary to know about students' social, psychological, and moral development in order to instruct, interact, teach discipline, and enforce rules.

Getting to Know Students

Just as the first few days of the school year are important to establishing rules and setting the classroom climate, it is also important to learn everything you can about the students. First, make it a point to learn their names as quickly as possible. If you teach young children, you may want to put a name label on each child's desk. This not only helps you know the child, but it may also help the child recognize his or her own name.

Effective classroom managers know students and let students know them.

When you teach large numbers of students, remembering names is not easy, and the more quickly you learn students' names, the more quickly they will feel they belong in your class. Many teachers devise clever ways of identifying students; for example, they make a seating chart for each class. This allows you to call on a student by name and look at the student simultaneously. A teacher who does not recognize a student by name has no relationship with that student. You may let students know that it is important to you to know their names and ask them to help you remember them in some way. Until you know a student's name, he or she is an "it;" no student should be an "it." Learning names can be turned into a spelling or memory game. Some teachers ask older students to give the ethnic origin of their surnames and at the same time gather information about students' backgrounds. You might have older students write a "get acquainted paper" in which they relate some things about themselves, such as hobbies, travel experiences, work experiences, family, favorite activities, and pet peeves.

During the first day or days of school, when you are teaching rules and procedures, you may want to plan "get acquainted time." This may be especially important in schools where the student population is mobile and changes frequently. Some students may be strangers to the community as well as to the school. Activities that help them find a friend at school are always worth the effort. Schedule activities that help students get to know each other and you, the teacher. Plan to tell students about yourself—not in great detail (don't tell your personal problems), but about such things as your embarrassing, difficult, or interesting school experiences. These stories help students see you as human. One senior high school teacher brings her college yearbooks and shares her required courses, major, social clubs, and so on. This gives students not only information about the teacher but also gives a preview of college life.

Form 3.8 WAYS TO LET STUDENTS KNOW YOU

1. Have sense of humor. Laugh when you feel like laughing—at situations, not at students.
2. Say "Hello" to students.
3. Talk with students during "break" times.
4. Stay with them when special occasions or incidents arise.
5. Introduce them to your family, through pictures or for real.
6. Tell them about a pet you have.
7. Share a collection of things you have.
8. Tell them about one of your favorite people, places, colors, books, and so on.
9. Share a happy or sad experience.
10. Share a school experience; for example, "I never liked to read until I read *Pippi Longstocking*," or "I used to read comic books or the *Hardy Boys*," or "I remember being the smallest girl/boy in my class."
11. Share your interests when they are relevant: "I like historical novels made into movies."
12. "I went to _____ College because _____ ."
13. "When I was in high school, the hottest fashion was _____ ."
14. Don't talk about yourself, your family, or your own life or interests too much. You may tell them more than they want to know.

Observe nonverbal behaviors such as how students enter the room, slouching in seats, general body posture, grooming, use of hands and feet, and so on, and certainly listen to the speech of your students. Language can be the single most revealing facet of any person. It communicates our culture, our intelligence, and our self-esteem. Listen to it! (See Form 3.9.)

Try to find something positive about each student. You may even want to record for your own use a positive statement about each student you teach. If you work with students about whom you find it particularly difficult to find something positive, make a special effort

Form 3.9 SOURCES OF INFORMATION ABOUT STUDENTS

1. *The student*: Always ask the student about his or her behavior, and provide time and create circumstances when and where students can communicate.
2. *The teacher observations*: Not all teacher observations are accurate. We sometimes see what we want to see. Check your biases and try to make sure you are accurately viewing and hearing students, but do be observant and sensitive to students' behavior.
3. *Other teachers and students*: Check your observations with those of others who observe the students.
4. *The parents*: The way the student behaves at home can provide insights into behavior at school. Parents' observations should always be considered; however, both parents and teachers can be biased in their views of student behavior.

to get to know these students better. You will find that there is something positive about each one. You have simply not recognized it. You may also find it difficult to recognize and admit any negative feelings you may have about some of your students, but the fact remains that you will like some students more than others. Ask yourself, "Why do I feel this way?" Also ask, "Do I really know this student?" Thoughtful teachers who are really concerned about students will use a variety of methods to know and understand students. Some of these methods, which are available to all teachers, are:

1. Moving about among students as they work and play.
2. Giving the children a chance to tell how they feel about things, what they are interested in, and what they are worried about through informal conversations.
3. Maintaining a warm, friendly, open atmosphere during group conversations and encouraging students to talk.
4. Getting acquainted with parents early in the year and planning ways in which you can work together to help each student as needed.
5. Planning ways to teach children how to be accepted as a group member.

Observant teachers will know such things as:

1. Who is the leader?
2. Which one makes helpful suggestions?
3. Who always wants his or her own way?

4. Who is willing to take turns?
5. Who seems to be left out?
6. Who seems listless and inattentive?
7. Who has poor work habits?
8. Who has good work habits?
9. What type of home life is the child experiencing?
10. Whose parents would I be least prepared to talk with about their child?
11. Who will react to certain situations in predictable or unpredictable ways?
12. Who needs attention?
13. Who wants to be left alone?
14. Who will follow the rules on his or her own initiative?
15. Who will need help with compliance?

As you get to know something about each student, ask yourself if you are or were in any way similar to your students. Were you ever "boy crazy" or "girl crazy"? Were you ever embarrassed by another student? Did you ever "goof off" and not do your homework? As a teacher you can empathize to some degree with students, but total empathy and complete understanding of students is impossible; and playing psychiatrist can be dangerous. The role of students is always different from the role of the teacher. Nevertheless, it is the teacher's responsibility at all times to understand as much as possible the views of students and their world. And of course, you should try to help students understand your views.

Knowing these things and more is crucial to developing student motivation and self-discipline. Rules and regulations will be more readily accepted, followed, and, if necessary, will be enforced more easily when teachers and students have some knowledge of the personal visions of each other. Knowledge and understanding can diminish the adversarial relationship of teachers and students and foster teacher-student alliances.

Caring about Students

A classroom environment where teacher and students are friends and friendly, respected and respectful, listened to and listen, understood and understand, epitomizes the complexity and fragility of a diverse group of individuals working toward a myriad of goals. The teacher who creates and maintains this amazingly delicate but sturdy and workable atmosphere where rules are willingly obeyed must be a fully informed and willing participant in all aspects of individual and group interactions (Brophy and Putnam, 1978). Such a teacher must care about students, and students must know the teacher cares.

> Effective classroom managers care about students and students know they care.

A major reason for students' dislike of school is the perception that nobody in the school knows them or cares about them. A recent research study indicates that students' attitudes toward school become increasingly negative by the time they reach ninth grade, and regardless of gender or ability level students perceive they have less interaction with the teacher as they progress through the grades. Students' perception of their personal interactions with teachers is a major influence on their attitudes toward school (Berliner, 1985). In a case study approach to investigating gifted students who dropped out of high school Sadowski (1987) found that all his subjects perceived most of their teachers as unavailable, aloof, and uninvolved. One college honors student, who was not a high school dropout and not a behavior problem and who thought she "belonged," told the author that when she returned to her high school after being ill for several days, not one of her teachers commented about her absence or return to class. (See Form 3.10.)

Form 3.10 BEHAVIORS THAT TELL STUDENTS TEACHERS CARE

1. Smile at them.
2. Touch them with spontaneity and care.
3. Make eye contact with them.
4. Listen to them.
5. Agree with them when possible.
6. Share your feelings and experiences with them.
7. Tell them what you expect.
8. Encourage them.
9. Praise them when it is merited.
10. Withhold critical remarks.
11. Ask them about themselves.

12. Laugh with them.
13. Ask for their opinions.
14. Notice something special about each student.
15. Set guidelines and rules.
16. Speak with each student individually each day.
17. When students share a personal concern with you, follow up at a later time with a question or comment that shows your concern and that you have not forgotten.
18. When students are absent because of illness, ask about their health when they return and/or call their house to inquire.
19. Remember, it is nice to wish them a happy birthday privately.
20. When you notice a change in behavior, let the student know you are aware; for example, you might comment to a student who is unusually quiet, that she or he is unusually quiet today. Notice if she or he is in a "bad mood" or had good news to share.
21. Greet students at the door with "good morning," or, "Hello."
22. Know students' names and use them.
23. When a student has been absent for a few days, find out why.
24. Give feedback on students' papers.
25. Give personalized, individual help whenever possible.
26. Conference with students; let them know you want them to achieve.
27. Be persistent and convey to problem students you will not "give up" on them.
28. Go to school events—sporting, musical, social events.
29. Call parents to tell them about a good deed or good work.
30. Use a kind voice.
31. Acknowledge eye contact and look them in the eye.
32. Acknowledge students when you see them outside the classroom.
33. Stop what you are doing and listen to them.
34. Talk with students about their work and their interests.
35. Write comments on papers which show you really read what they wrote.
36. Accept their opinions as worthy of thought.
37. Trust and don't always assume a student is wrong.
38. Notice when students are different, for example, arm in sling, dramatically different hair cut.
39. Notice when a student seems to be having trouble and offer to assist.
40. Loan them pencils, lunch money, and so on when, on rare occasions, they are needed.
41. Use humor on occasion to lighten up.
42. Have appropriate expectations for students.
43. Be available for students who need your help.
44. Be prepared to teach them.

Caring about students means we attend to their needs— social and psychological as well as academic. Showing that you care can be as complex as helping students cope with a major problem at home or as simple as giving a student a smile. Caring means we do not ignore students' needs. For example, if you teach in a secondary school, you may have a student who never has materials for class participation, such as a book and a pencil. As a result the student sits quietly, perhaps without acknowledgement of this predicament, and doesn't seem to care or be disturbed about this state of affairs. When a class activity is assigned, the student will state that he or she cannot participate for lack of materials and seems to be both agitated and delighted with the circumstances. This can be absolutely maddening for the teacher. If you ignore the student, he or she cannot participate and learn; however, you can get drawn into a daily ritual of finding the student a book and a pencil, which delays the entire class and consumes the learning time of all students. What can be done?

First, talk with the student privately. Ask if he or she possesses a book and pencil. If so, where are they? Why are they not brought to class? You may be surprised to find some validity in the student's answers. Whatever the reason, don't get drawn into a daily "big deal" routine of publicly asking "why" and finding the materials. Instead, plan ahead for this student. Get a copy of the book and a pencil, which can be quietly given to the student at the beginning of the period, and inform the student that the book and pencil must be returned at the end of the class period. You should not plan to do this for the entire year. Continue to conference with the student. It is possible that at some point the student will take responsibility for bringing his or her own materials.

Some teachers argue they should not have to go to such lengths to help students. True! This should not be necessary. But ask yourself, "Shall I let this student's behavior interfere with the entire class? What will be the results if I do or if I do not go the extra mile? Am I the adult and should I model appropriate behavior, or shall I feel sorry for myself that I have such irresponsible, immature, or academically deficient students in my class?" Remember, teachers are responsible for students' learning. Be assured that when you know and can understand the students' behavior, your chances for helping them increase. Most students are generally more likely to cooperate with teachers and follow the rules if they think teachers care about them as people as well as students. However, this is not always true, and beginning teachers should realize that caring about students will not automatically secure their confidence, trust, and cooperation. Unfortunately, some students have not learned to trust and care about others and themselves. Some students have serious emotional problems and may need professional psychological help. Behavior problems, and all students' problems, cannot always be resolved by caring teachers, but letting students know you care is still important. Plan to show students that you care (Smuck and Smuck, 1979).

Thus far in our discussion of preventing management and discipline problems we have said that effective managers establish rules, procedures, and routines that prevent many inappropriate behaviors. We have also said that rules alone will not ensure appropriate student behavior, and that knowing students is essential to effective management and discipline because until we know students, we cannot be assured that our rules and general procedures for teaching and learning together are appropriate and functional. Planning for preventing management and discipline problems can be done only in terms of general human behavior until we know and understand our students as individuals and as a group. In truth, we cannot effectively plan for students we do not know, but we can plan and enforce rules, procedures, and routines that prevent many inappropriate behaviors when we know and care about students.

Effective managers create a classroom climate that encourages desirable behavior and enhances students' ability to discipline themselves. A significant characteristic of this climate is that teachers know and care about their students. Effective managers also demonstrate specific behaviors that tell students that they not only know and care about students but that they also act on this knowledge. Two of these behaviors are teacher "with-it-ness" and monitoring.

Exhibiting With-It-ness

The teacher who knows students, is attentive to what is happening in the classroom, and can anticipate and predict student behavior is a with-it teacher (Kounin, 1970). Research findings indicate that those with-it teachers, whom students describe as having eyes in the back of their heads, have fewer discipline problems than teachers who do not know about students.

Effective classroom managers exhibit with-it-ness.

Effective managers *observe, know, anticipate,* and *communicate* to students that they know about them. In other words, they are in the center of what is happening in their classrooms. They are not outsiders. They are insiders and are "with" the action. Students realize that the with-it teacher is involved and aware, that is, not easy to fool, will know what is happening, will suspect, has eyes in the back of his or her head, and will act on information.

You may recall with-it teachers you have encountered. They may have been called "eagle eye," Sherlock Holmes, or some other nickname that indicated that these teachers were knowledgeable about classroom interactions. You have also probably encountered teachers who seemed to know or anticipate little about students and classroom happenings. These teachers could be fooled, could have the wool pulled over their eyes, and would believe anything or nothing. Unfortunately, some teachers fail to recognize—much less understand and plan to manage—the complexities of group and individual interactions in classrooms. With-it-ness enables the teacher to anticipate student behavior, which in turn makes it possible to plan for prevention of misbehavior.

Kounin's research findings also indicated that successful classroom managers could attend to more than one classroom happening at a time. He called this ability to manage two or more situations simultaneously "overlapping." His studies also indicate that "momentum," the presence or absence of slow-downs in the pace of instructional activities, influences student behavior. Effective managers keep the momentum of instructional activities moving so that students' attention is demanded. Such teachers are able to prevent disruptions that slow down activities and provide opportunities for misconduct. Momentum, overlapping, and with-it-ness appear to be strongly related to effective management and can be planned (Evertson and Emmer, 1982b; Weber, et al., 1983).

Monitoring

Maintaining momentum and using overlapping and other with-it-ness behaviors requires skillful and purposeful observation and monitoring of behavior. Careful monitoring can prevent inappropriate behavior as well as ensure desired behavior. It is not only an important and necessary activity for preventing disorder, but it is also important for maximizing students' attention to learning, which is discussed in Chapter 4.

Effective classroom managers monitor to prevent problems.

With-it teachers are cognizant of potential student actions and reactions and that students' behavior can be influenced by simply letting them know that you are anticipating and aware of possible thoughts, intentions, and actions. Successful classroom managers plan to monitor students' behavior carefully and purposefully. Monitoring not only alerts the teacher to stop misbehavior promptly but also prevents undesirable behavior. The following tips for monitoring are based on those of researchers Emmer, et al. (1983):

1. Stand where you can see the entire class when you are making presentations, giving directions, and so on.
2. Scan the room frequently. Don't focus on one student or a few students who may be attentive or even inattentive.
3. When students are doing seatwork or working on projects or assignments, move around the room and check for student progress and understanding. Don't let one or two students or a group of students consume your attention so that you lose contact with what others are doing. An example of this phenomenon is one beginning teacher who divided a fourth grade class into five groups to work on a poster for a schoolwide contest. He told the class he would come to each group to give details and assist. In fact, he spent 20 minutes of the 40 minute language arts period with the first group of students. The remaining groups (25 students) were left to wait for the teacher. As a result disorder and boredom reigned. Students in the first group were even distracted by the disorder, but the teacher kept to his original plan.
4. Permit only one or two students to come to your desk at one time. Groups of students around the teacher's desk block your vision of the entire room.
5. Assist the entire class with the first problem or question brought

up by seatwork assignments. You can determine if everyone is working and able to do the assignment.

When teachers know their students, they are often able to anticipate behaviors, to monitor, and to plan to prevent those behaviors. For example, when you know that a particular student will need some help with a project, with solving a problem in science or mathematics, or with finding a special reference, you can go to that student and assist before she or he becomes agitated. When you know there is some conflict between students A and B, you can avoid calling on student B to comment on A's answer. When you observe that student C has a crush on student D, you can give them opportunities to socialize in constructive ways. When you see that a student is about to explode with anger or laughter, a look or touch can often defuse the action. Touching is a personal and delicate behavior; its use requires astute judgment and knowledge of students. Some students will react to touch with hostility; they view touching as an invasion of their space. However, when students know the teacher and understand touch as a gentle expression of restraint or praise, it can be a powerful and effective communication, especially if it is spontaneous.

SUMMARY

You have discerned by now that many inappropriate behaviors can be prevented and that effective managers *plan* to prevent management problems and teach discipline.

Principles of effective management discussed in this chapter are that effective managers *plan* and

1. organize their classrooms and materials,
2. establish rules and procedures prior to or at the beginning of the school year,
3. teach rules and procedures,
4. create a classroom climate that encourages compliance with rules and procedures,
5. know students and let students know them,
6. exhibit with-it-ness, and
7. monitor to prevent problems.

Of course, many behaviors and activities other than those listed in this chapter can prevent misbehavior and can be planned. For example, maximizing student attention to learning prevents behavior problems and must also be planned. Behaviors of teachers that can maximize students' attention will be discussed in Chapter 4.

QUESTIONS AND ACTIVITIES

3.1 Look carefully at a classroom at your college or school. Draw a seating arrangement that would be appropriate for the age and grade level of students who are currently using the room or for the age and grade level you are currently teaching.

3.2 Make a list of materials you think you will need at the beginning of the school year. Look at the classroom seating arrangement and the storage spaces you have planned. Anticipate traffic patterns and decide where you will store your materials.

3.3 Choose content and skills you would teach during the first month of the school year. Outline a plan for a bulletin board or displays you will want in your room. You can save time and energy by saving materials and retooling them for future teaching.

3.4 Make a list of five or six rules for a class you currently teach or plan to teach. Remember the age level, the kind of classroom climate you want, and the rules for writing rules.

3.5 Choose one or two of your colleagues and discuss your list of rules with them. Identify possible problems or pitfalls and if necessary restate the rules more appropriately.

3.6 If you are currently enrolled in a college class, make a list of procedures you are expected to follow. Do you think these procedures facilitate or hinder the operation of the class?

3.7 If you are student teaching or have a class of your own, list the procedures your students are expected to follow. What do you think of these procedures? Are they needed? Are there any problems in this classroom that a routine procedure might help diminish?

3.8 Look carefully at Forms 3.1, 3.2, 3.3, 3.4, and 3.5. What do you like about these rules and procedures? What do you dislike? What are some of the differences in this group of rules? Why are grade level differences important?

3.9 Why do students need rules? Make a list of reasons.

3.10 List characteristics of a "good" rule.

3.11 Why are rules not followed?

3.12 List aspects of student behavior that can be planned for that are discussed in this chapter.

3.13 This chapter provides many general and specific suggestions for planning to prevent inappropriate behavior. List some other specific behaviors that might be planned for.

3.14 Develop a plan to teach a rule. Follow guidelines suggested.

3.15 If all the measures for preventing inappropriate behavior fail, what happens? What do effective managers do next? (You will find some of the answers in the following chapters.)

3.16 Do you believe there is a recipe for preventing behavior problems? Why or why not?

3.17 Make a list of the principles suggested in Chapters 2 and 3 for securing appropriate student behavior. Which principle do you think will be most difficult to implement? Why? Which will be easiest? Why?

3.18 Write a description of the "best" teacher you ever had. Why do you remember this teacher so vividly? What principles discussed in this chapter did this teacher use?

3.19 *Writing rules*: The following rules do not meet one or more criteria for appropriate rules. Tell the criteria that are not met and restate the rule in an appropriate way.

    (a) Don't lean back in your chairs.

    (b) Due to the fact that the school budget for materials has been spent, you should use supplies sparingly.

    (c) Don't use the restrooms when another person is there.

    (d) Be quiet and orderly in the halls.

    (e) Students who do the best work will be allowed library privileges.

3.20 *Writing specific behaviors that clarify general rules*: General rules that cover broad areas of behavior sometimes need to be translated into specific observable behaviors. Look at rule A for an example, and then specify four behaviors for each of the remaining rules.

    Rule A: Clean up work areas when your work is completed.
    Behaviors:

1. Put leftover supplies in proper storage place.

2. Pick up any trash produced.

3. Put finished work on teacher's desk or other designated place.

4. Wipe up any liquids spilled.

    Rule B: Respect others and their property.

    Rule C: You may move from your seat only when necessary.

    Rule D: Work quietly.

    Rule E: Be prepared to begin work when the bell rings.

REFERENCES

Berliner, D. (1985). "Can We Help Children Stay Enthusiastic about School?" *Instructor*. XCIV (2), pp. 12–13.

Brophy, J., and Good, T. (1986). "Teacher Behavior and Student Achievement." In M. Wittrock (ed.) *Handbook of Research on Teaching* (3rd ed.). New York: Macmillan.

Brophy, J., and Putnam, J. (1978). *Classroom Management in the Elementary Grades*. (Research Series 32). East Lansing, Mich.: Michigan State University, Institute for Research on Teaching.

Doyle, W. (1986). "Classroom Organization and Management." In M. Wittrock (ed.). *Handbook of Research on Teaching* (3rd ed.). New York: Macmillan.

Emmer, E., Evertson, C., and Anderson, L. (1980). "Effective Classroom Management at the Beginning of the School Year." *Elementary School Journal*, *80* (5), pp. 219–231.

Emmer, E., Evertson, C., Stanford, J., Clements, B., and Worsham, M. (1989). *Classroom Management for Secondary Students* (2nd ed.). Englewood Cliffs, N.J.: Prentice-Hall.

Emmer, E., et al. (1983). *Organizing and Managing the Junior High Classroom*. (R and D No. 6151). Austin, Tex.: University of Texas Research and Development Center for Teacher Education, pp. 95–96.

Evertson, C., and Emmer, E. (1982a). "Effective Management at the Beginning of the School Year in Junior High Classes." *Journal of Educational Psychology*, *74*, pp. 485–498.

Evertson, C., and Emmer, E. (1982b). "Preventive Classroom Management." In D. Duke (ed.) *Helping Teachers Manage Classrooms*. Alexandria, Va.: Association for Supervision and Curriculum Development.

Evertson, C., Emmer, E., Clements, B., Sanford, J., and Worsham, M. (1989). *Classroom Management for Elementary Teachers* (2nd ed.). Englewood Cliffs, N.J.: Prentice-Hall.

Hunter, M., and Barker, G. (1987). "'If at first . . . ': Attribution theory in the classroom." *Educational Leadership*, 45 (2), pp. 50–53.

Kohlberg, L., and Turiel, E. (1971). *Research in Moral Development: A Cognitive Developmental Approach*. New York: Holt, Rinehart, and Winston.

Kounin, J. (1970). *Discipline and Group Management in Classrooms*. New York: Rinehart and Winston.

Nucci, L. (1987). "Synthesis of Research on Moral Development." *Educational Leadership*, *44* (5), pp. 86–92.

Piaget, J. (1932). *The Moral Judgment of the Child*. London: Kegan and Paul.

Sadowski, A. (1987). *A Case Study of the Experiences of and Influences upon Gifted High School Dropouts*. Unpublished doctoral dissertation. Coral Gables, Fla.: University of Miami.

Smuck, R., and Smuck, P. (1979). *Group Processes in the Classroom*. Dubuque, Iowa: William C. Brown.

Squires, D., Huitt, W., and Segars, J. (1984). *Effective Schools and Effective Classrooms: A Research Based Perspective*. Alexandria, Va.: Association for Supervision and Curriculum Development.

Warren, R. (1977). *Caring: Supporting Children's Growth*. Washington, D.C.: National Association for the Education of Young Children.

Weber, W., Crawford, J., Roff, L., and Robinson, C. (1983). *Classroom Management: Reviews of the Teacher Education and Research Literature*. Princeton, N.J.: Educational Testing Service.

Chapter
4

Maximizing Student Attention

The fundamental reason why children do not act right is because they do not have the conditions for right action.

Frances W. Parker

INTRODUCTION AND OBJECTIVES

The old adage, "An idle mind is the devil's workshop," appears to be true in classrooms. Researchers have found that when students spend a major portion of their time actively engaged in learning, there are fewer disruptive behaviors than when time is idly frittered away with little or no attention to learning. But which comes first, active learning or appropriate behavior? There is obvious truth in the remark a student teacher made to her supervisor: "I could teach if they (students) would let me." Many teachers with disruptive classes never seen able to demonstrate their ability to teach, and they must be able to teach in order to manage behavior successfully. Researchers and successful, experienced teachers think that in classrooms with major discipline problems teachers are unable to enforce rules and establish authority because they fail to provide interesting and worthwhile instruction.

In classrooms where discipline is a major problem, teachers often have virtually no variety in lesson plans, rarely encourage students to explore the significance of the learning task, and rarely evaluate learning. On the other hand, research findings indicate that successful managers view student learning as a central objective, and they therefore take planning for instruction seriously. They realize that the starting point for securing appropriate student behavior is a carefully planned and skillfully executed lesson. They also understand that it is more advantageous and more productive to invest effort in good instruction than in punishing and reprimanding bored students. Effective class-room managers realize the importance of focusing student attention to learning tasks.

Effective classroom managers maximize student attention and participation.

Many teachers are sometimes unaware of what goes on in typical classrooms. They are not cognizant of their own actions and do not understand students' behavior. They sometimes erroneously believe that they deliver interesting and appropriate information and instruc-tion. They often think that classroom problems reside in children and not within specific environments and specific situations. Preservice teachers tend to believe that the children involved can control their social immaturity and social defiance; they hold children responsible for their own conduct. It is difficult for some teachers to realize that undesirable behavior of students may not be due to students' social immaturity but may be a result of learning conditions. The teacher must observe and be aware of behavior that indicates problems with any aspect of the classroom environment, including instruction.

The Office of Staff Development of Dade County, Florida, Public Schools (1984), fourth largest school system in the United States, alerts beginning teachers to indicators of possible problems with instruction. Teachers are told that instructional problems can be manifested by such academic indicators as:

low or declining test scores,
frequent wrong answers on practice exercises,
frequent wrong answers on homework assignments,
incomplete practice exercise frequently handed in,
refusal to do practice exercises,
refusal to do homework assignments,
hesitation before trying to answer questions in class, and
little or no voluntary participation in lesson activities.

Students will make such comments as:

"I didn't have enough time."
"I didn't understand lots of the English words."
"I lost my book."
"I forgot my pencil."
"This was just too hard."
"I don't understand this stuff."
"Will you go over it again, slower?"
"I can't write down what you say fast enough."

During instruction students will:

write a letter, note, and so one;
read a library book;
work on assignments for another class;
draw or doodle;
stare at the ceiling or out the window;
put head on desk (sometimes dozing off);
not "know the place" when called upon;
throw paper, chalk, pencils, and so on;
get out of seats;
blurt out a comment;
tap feet;
talk to other students;
call out your name to get attention;
hit, push, or shove other students; or
grab possessions of other students.[1]

Even though teachers may not be aware of the reasons for inattention, they certainly recognize the problem. When beginning secondary teachers were asked to identify and describe their biggest management problem, they wrote the following:

Teacher 1

My most frequent discipline problems are constant talking, incessant inattention, inability to stay seated, and failure to carry out orders.

---

[1]Reprinted from Bureau of Staff Development, *Classroom Management*.

There exists a small group whose sole purpose in school is to be disruptive. It's usually a group of students who know each other and are organized into a well-oiled talking machine.

Teacher 2

One of the largest problems I have occurring in class is that of not paying attention. Many times during class, I need to stop what's happening in class and get them back on task. I realize that many outside distractions cause students to be thinking about other things. I have seen an abnormally high incidence of tardiness recently. I have attributed this to the holidays being upon us.

Teacher 3

I teach mathematics. The most common problem, especially during my Algebra I class, is that they [students] want to talk while I am teaching at the board. These students do not understand the reason for taking Algebra I. They would much rather "tune out" the teaching lesson. They also engage in name-calling. When a student answers a question incorrectly, I would prefer that we work together and try to correct his or her mistake. However, some students would rather inform their incorrect classmate of his mental capabilities. They proclaim "You dummy," "You don't know anything," and so on.

Teacher 4

Some of the discipline problems that I've been experiencing have been the following: disruptive behavior due to the constant talking without permission, getting up to throw paper away or to sharpen pencils, screaming from one person to the other person on the other side of the room, and the negative attitudes that the students show when they are reprimanded. They become aggressive and defensive if you tell them something or punish them for some behavior. Those that cause me the most stress are the ones that refuse to do any work and still ask, "Why am I failing?" I have a great problem in motivating these students to study and to pay attention.

Teacher 5

Students talking during lectures, during book work or any deskwork assignments; breaking into utter pandemonium if I sit at my desk and therefore am not looking at them. Student talking includes students blurting out an answer, either before they have been called on when raising hands or without raising hands. Students not remaining in their seats. They stand up and come to me to ask questions because they get impatient waiting for me to come around to them.

Although it is not possible to say with certainty that any one or several of these behaviors indicate that instruction, content, and materials are inappropriate, these behaviors do support a reasonable hypothesis that they may be a source of at least some of the problems cited by teachers and the Dade County Office of Staff Development.

During the 1976–78 school year John Goodlad (1984) conducted "a study of schooling" in America. His study describes American education as routine, superficial, and flat. He found little variety in teaching practices, that teachers spend the majority of class time lecturing to classes and students spend most of their time working on written assignments such as seatwork. The most common pattern of instruction was the teacher lecturing to a total class or to a single student, asking factual questions, or monitoring.

A major objective of all teachers should be to make instruction interesting and challenging—not flat. The purpose of this chapter is to address teaching behaviors that can maximize student attention and participation, thus minimizing the flatness of many classrooms and providing an atmosphere of excitement in which students learn academics and self-discipline.

In Chapter 4 we discuss selected aspects of effective instruction that maximize student attention to tasks and thus minimize inappropriate student behavior. After completing a thorough study of this chapter, you will be able to

- describe and demonstrate teacher behaviors that get students' attention;
- choose appropriate methods for maximizing students' attention when given a teaching situation and classroom environment;
- give examples of teacher behaviors that maximize students' learning time;
- describe students' responses to realistic and unrealistic expectations;
- describe students' responses to appropriate and inappropriate levels of instruction;
- list teacher behaviors that monitor independent seatwork activities and maximize students' attention;
- suggest an appropriate seatwork activity and time block for achieving an instructional goal;
- characterize effective and appropriate pacing of instruction;
- characterize effective and appropriate feedback and give examples;

- list ways of getting students to participate;
- tell how a teacher's attitude toward teaching and learning can maximize students' attention;
- list and demonstrate ways to maximize students' attention, and;
- plan for maximizing student attention.

GETTING AND HOLDING STUDENTS' ATTENTION

You have already learned the importance of planning for the first few days of the school year. You can set the tone for the kind of classroom you want by communicating and modeling respect for students, the value and joy of learning, consistency, credibility, dependability, and responsibility for learning. In order to model and communicate these qualities, you must get students' attention; this must be done quickly and decisively, at the beginning of the school year, on the first day or even in the first ten minutes of the class.

Effective classroom managers get and hold students' attention.

The way you begin a lesson each day is just as important as the way you being the first day of the school year. Teachers should communicate that they expect every student's attention every day and throughout the lesson; therefore, do not begin teaching until you have everyone's attention. You can gain attention by signals such as raising or clapping your hands, rapping on your desk, or simply saying, "We are ready to begin." Wait until students are quiet; do not try to talk loudly or yell to be heard. If some students are slow to respond, call them by name. A good first comment may be a question, a statement of the objective, or a review statement. Whatever it is, follow with relevant, interesting comments enthusiastically presented. The more naturally enthusiastic and interested you appear, the more likely students' attention will be focused on the lesson.

In many, if not most, classrooms the teacher is the principal stimulus for students' attention to task. Therefore varying your teaching behavior can enhance attention. Some dimensions of behavior that might be varied are your volume or quality of voice, rate of speech, gestures, body position, position in the classroom, use of teaching aids, pacing of the lesson, assignments, and method of presentation.

Even though the teacher has a well planned lesson and presents it in an interesting manner, rarely are all students attending to learning; the learner who attends all the time is rare. Students who are attending should be reinforced by such things as smiles, comments, being called on, and verbal feedback. Similarly, students who fail to attend need redirection, and a different stimulus must be provided. When problems of inattention occur in spite of careful planning, teachers need to analyze students' behavior and their own carefully. They should identify those students who are attentive and those who are not. After a careful analysis of all available information relative to these students and careful, purposeful observation, teachers should be able to describe the problem of inattention in an objective manner and formulate a plan for solving the problem. (Examples of planning for solving problems can be found in this chapter and in chapter 7.)

UTILIZING TIME

Establishing the classroom climate for carrying on the business of teaching and learning includes the use of time. Researchers tell us that effective teachers and managers use the time allocated for learning efficiently and effectively. Maximizing students' time on task not only increases student achievement but also minimizes disruptive behavior.

Effective classroom managers maximize students' opportunities to learn by effectively and efficiently utilizing the time allocated for learning.

Effective managers view time as a valuable resource instead of hours and minutes to wile away. Their view of time is, "We have so little time to learn all these skills and information. I must plan carefully and utilize the time wisely." On the other hand, some teachers' view of time is, "We have a long school day. What can I do to fill up the day or the period?"

Schools are bound by the calendar and the clock. Generally speaking, elementary schools operate from 8:30 A.M. to 3:00 P.M., secondary schools from 7:30 A.M. to 2:30 P.M., and the academic school year is 180 days. Researchers indicate that the amount of this time spent on learning tasks is positively related to achievement; however, not all time allocated to instruction is devoted to instruction. In some classrooms a large portion of the allocated time is spent on discipline, management, routines, and other activities. Research findings demonstrate that the time students spend engaged in learning with a high success rate varies enormously from teacher to teacher. This engaged time with a high success rate, called *academic learning time* (ALT), influences achievement positively (Stallings, 1980). It goes without saying, then, that if teachers spend large amounts of allocated time securing order, less time will be available for learning and that if students learn, they must have time and opportunity to learn.

Effective managers ensure students an opportunity to learn by seeing to it that a large proportion of school time that is allocated for instruction is actually used for instruction. Effective teaching and managerial behaviors and activities that contribute to instructional time include routinizing procedures, minimizing transition time between class activities, beginning instruction on time, pacing, monitoring, and ensuring the quality of instruction (Wyne and Stuck, 1983).

In Chapter 3 it was suggested that establishing and teaching rules and procedures provides a basis for a good beginning. Planning, establishing routines, and enforcing rules and procedures also help make possible effective and efficient use of time. In addition to streamlining routines, the teacher should begin and end classwork on time. Getting going when the bell rings indicates to students that you think the work is important and that their time is valuable. It also indicates that you take learning seriously and expect the same from them. You do not stop instruction ten minutes early because you have "run out of things to do." Remember, there are so many things to be taught and learned that serious-minded teachers and students never have enough time. Your approach to time, in truth, communicates your attitude toward learning and your expectations of students.

A general guideline for effective and efficient use of time is: Most of the period/day is devoted to some form of instruction rather than to organization, management, and discipline. This means (1) instructional activities should begin promptly, (2) there should be no unnecessary delays during instruction, (3) transitions from one activity or class to another should be smooth, and (4) instructional activities should continue until the end of the period. (See Form 4.1.) Unfortunately, some teachers with disruptive classes never seem able to establish enough order to teach. Disruptive students can and do consume the instructional time of their teachers and the potential learning time of their peers.

Form 4.1 DECREASING DISRUPTIONS AND INCREASING TIME FOR LEARNING

1. Assign seats to students. This enables you to take roll quickly. Secondary teachers will find a seating chart for each class helpful.
2. Discuss problems common to many or most students in class. Address individual student problems before or after class.
3. Use student helpers and monitors to collect papers and distribute materials.
4. Give each student a written copy of directions for any assignments that are long, complicated, or extended for more than one day.
5. Have students correct short quiz papers in class.
6. Give students detailed and adequate instructions for preparing special papers or reports.
7. Make certain all students can hear you and other students.
8. Make certain all students can see demonstrations, materials, chalkboard, and so on.
9. Upper elementary and secondary teachers should give students specific objectives for units of instruction.
10. Primary and lower elementary teachers should write objectives on papers or on the chalkboard.

DETERMINING EXPECTATIONS

Effective teachers have realistic and appropriate expectations for student achievement and behavior. Researchers tell us that most inservice teachers have a pretty good idea of the level of work students can or cannot do (Brophy and Good, 1974). However, in spite of their valid assessment of student capabilities, many teachers continue to try to teach at levels beyond their students' ability to master and comprehend. They teach at grade levels instead of student levels, and as a consequence, students misbehave.

Effective classroom managers hold appropriate and realistic expectations for students' achievement and behavior.

A common manifestation of unrealistically high expectations is teachers assigning independent and supervised work that is above students' achievement levels. Research findings indicate that average students need an 80 percent success rate for effective learning to take place, and that for low achieving students the success rate should be around 90 percent. However, it is a common practice of many teachers to assign work, particularly seatwork, that students cannot read or comprehend. A study of reading seatwork by Anderson, et al. (1985) showed that students spend 30 to 60 percent of reading instruction time doing seatwork and that an average of 50 percent of each assignment utilized commercially prepared materials.

In many classrooms students cannot read seatwork materials, see no relevance to their learning, and fail to complete the work. It is not surprising, then, that research studies also reveal that the primary goal of low achieving students is to get seatwork "done," not necessarily to get it right. It seems obvious that if assignments are inappropriate or too difficult, students will be bored, apathetic, frustrated, and finally disruptive. Yet teachers continue to give assignments that are too difficult and expect students to be attentive to task. Remember, when students succeed they are more apt to cooperate with school rules and procedures, behave appropriately, and in the end, develop some self-control and self-discipline.

Expectations of teachers can also be too low. Boredom and apathy can be signs of teachers' low expectations in many schools. Horace's Compromise, mentioned in Chapter 2, is the ultimate example of teachers' abdication of their responsibility for student learning; they expect little—just enough to be allowed to play the teacher's role—and they get little.

Somewhere between the teachers who expect minimum work and achievement from students and the teachers who make unrealistic demands and hold unrealistic expectations that all students be able to meet the same standards, there are teachers who hold realistic expectations and encourage students to perform at their levels of capability. These teachers believe students can learn and that they themselves can teach. They push students to do their best; they expect the best from students; and they get the best in both academic achievement and behavior. One of these teachers was described by a former student in the following way:

It has been ten years, and I am still talking about him. I look back on high school with a general resentment that I did not learn as much as I was capable of learning. There is no question in my mind that the better the student is in high school, the less effort she or he has to put out to keep up. No so in Mr. W.'s classes.

Mr. W. taught eleventh grade honors English, and I mean *taught*. Instead of assuming that we already knew enough and read enough and therefore hold a day care center for an hour each day, he prodded us, hammered at us, criticized our work, patted us on the back (occasionally), and taught with his whole being, inspired us, awed us, and pushed us to our limits.

Whoever heard of a test every Monday morning? What else are Mondays good for? Thirty pages a night and then a quiz each day on the assignment. How about an essay due every other day for two weeks? But we did it. We were proud. We were learning. Everything had its purpose and we knew it. The objectives and goals for the year were clearly put forth from the very beginning. We were going to learn expository writing and American literature. We did.

Students asked him why he was teaching high school. We felt he was too good for us. Why did he not get his Ph.D. and teach on the college level? Because he loved teaching *us*. We were special. Eleventh grade was his favorite, and honors classes were challenging.

The greatest compliment that I can offer to this teacher—his dedication, talent, and teaching ability—is that later it was proven that I did learn. I was prepared for college. Freshman English was a repetition and reinforcement of what I had learned in eleventh grade. I was grateful. I will never forget Mr. W.

An effective classroom is one in which goals are challenging and expectations are accurate, realistic, clearly understood, and accepted by the students. If teachers have appropriate expectations for their students and instruct and make assignments at appropriate levels, students will manifest more interest in learning, be less apathetic, spend more time on learning tasks, and be less disruptive. All too often when students are apathetic and disruptive, teachers try to deal with the problem by blaming students and trying to become tougher. They fail to deal with the fundamental root of the problem. One senior high history teacher described her biggest teaching and management problem in the following way:

> My most common teaching and discipline problem occurs with my Introduction to American History class. The class in general possesses an apathetic attitude which irks the instructor.
>
> Occasionally within the classroom setting, there are basic disturbances of talking or sudden outbursts of laughter. Although this occurs often in the basic class, it rarely occurs in the general American History classes.

The same teacher analyzed her introductory class and developed a plan to solve the problem. Note that apathy was not a problem in all the classes she taught—only in the introductory class. She thought about the problem and decided to do more than punish disruptive students. Her objective was to prevent apathy as well as disruptive behavior. She did not "give up" on this class or abandon her responsibility to teach. Instead she developed the following plan to resolve the problems.

PLAN FOR PREVENTING DISRUPTIVE BEHAVIOR

Long-range Objective:

The objective of this plan is to prevent disruptive behavior in the classroom by changing expectations and increasing academic learning time.

Problem: Disruptive behavior in the form of tardiness, apathy, and continuous talking.

Personal Reflections:

Many thoughts travel through one's mind in endeavoring to find a solution to this type of problem. But before one attempts to devise a solution, the problem must be totally understood by all those involved.

This form of disruptive behavior exists in a low level Introduction to American History course. There seems to be no behavior problems with my other classes. Why in this class? This question must be examined. It would be most expedient at this time to compare the nondisruptive classes with the disruptive class.

No Behavioral Problem	**Behavioral Problem**
Students are motivated	Students are apathetic
Students are high achievers	Students are low achievers
Courses are general/advanced	Course is low level introduction
Students follow directions	Students rarely complete tasks
Students are attentive	Students show low concentration levels

Solution: The solution is to develop teaching strategies and methods relevant to the needs of a low level class. This will facilitate an atmosphere conducive to learning and diminish disruptive behavior.

Solution Procedures:

Preliminary evaluations had to be made before new strategies could be implemented in the classroom.

1. Readability formulas were used to evaluate the grade level of the textbook.

Results: Formula I, 9.5 grade level
Formula II, 10.0 grade level

2. Cloze test administered to students.

Results: Reading levels varied
Lowest—not able to read English
Highest—11.0 grade level

Most students read on or slightly above seventh grade level.

3. Goal focusing and the nature of learning in this particular classroom was reevaluated. Students were having difficulty reading the text.

Conclusion: The material and activities needed for the content coverage would have to be modified to meet the various needs of the students.

Short-Range Goal:

The short-range goal/objective is to diminish the disruptive behavior occurring in the Introductory American History class (11th grade).

Day 1: The students will be retaught the classroom procedures and rules.

Daily Observations: Student behavior in general appeared to improve when these rules were enforced.

Day 2: *Instruction:* After instruction on the War of 1812 at students' level of understanding, most of the class will be able to list and discuss four causes that led to this war with Great Britain.

Behavior: During instruction the student will take notes and ask and answer questions pertaining to the material in focus.

Daily Observations: It was remarkable! The class was on task and there were only a few disruptions. With these guidelines, the students were active participants in learning. The second day was much better than the first. *Positive Progression.*

Day 3: After review of the causes of the War of 1812 the student will be able to evaluate these causes on three levels: associational, functional, and conceptual.

Daily Observations: The instruction was broken into small, distinct sets of questions on all three levels of learning. In evaluating student performance, the class was more comfortable and performed much better with "right and wrong" and "recognition-memory" questions.

Day 4: The student will evaluate his or her knowledge of the subject material in focus. An objective test consisting of multiple choice, matching, and short answer will be administered for this evaluation.

Daily Observations: The results of the test prove that this highly structured and supervised format of instructional behavior benefitted the students.

Day 5: The students will be introduced to new material through study, question, answer, and review.

Daily Observations: Through continuous, supervised monitoring and immediate feedback, the students stayed on task and performed on a higher level than previously.

Conclusion:
Disruptive behavior diminished by using the following instructional and behavioral strategies:

1. Workable, detailed lesson plans with instructional and **behavioral objectives**.

2. Short and frequent writing activities used as review and reinforcement of material.
3. Thoroughly covering material.
4. Positive feedback and specific praise for good performance.
5. Immediate and consistent response to negative, disruptive behavior.
6. Supervision of small group work activities thus increasing interactive instruction.
7. Short, frequent seatwork and homework assignments to reinforce material learned in class.
8. And most importantly, positive teacher attitude, flexibility, and humor.
9. Realistic goals and expectations.

The disruptive behavior as described in this study occurred during independent seatwork with activities too difficult for most students in the class to grasp. Thus, by modifying expectations and content of instruction, a pleasant atmosphere conducive for learning has been created.

Notice that in this plan the teacher focused on her teaching. When she changed expectations, content, instructional strategies, and attitude, students began to change, apathy decreased, student attention to task increased, and fewer disruptions occurred. This teacher found that the problem behavior was enhanced, if not directly caused, by the nature of the teaching and learning environment. She also found that when she changed the environment, student behavior changed. (See Form 4.2.) More examples of planning for preventing and resolving behavior problems can be found in Chapter 7.

Form 4.2 SOME THOUGHTS ON MAXIMIZING STUDENT ATTENTION

1. We can improve the quality of learning by becoming more sensitive to what goes on inside the student. We know the student is learning something. Is it what we want the student to learn?
2. Students must succeed more than they fail.
3. A high rate of success is important.
4. Set a standard that can be reached.
5. Go at a pace students can follow.
6. Plan for eliminating inappropriate and reinforcing appropriate behavior.

UTILIZING SEATWORK AND OTHER ASSIGNMENTS

> Effective classroom managers provide interesting, meaningful seatwork and monitor for understanding.

Teachers rely on seatwork activities to keep students busy while they work with small groups and individuals. Anderson, et al. (1985) found that when many teachers monitored seatwork, they emphasized keeping busy and completing the work rather than understanding. They seldom explained what students were to learn from doing the work and were more concerned about behavior than performance. Some elementary students spend a large percentage of their time doing seatwork, so it is not surprising that teachers are concerned about behavior during this activity.

One way to ensure students spend more time on task during seatwork is to shorten the length of each time block. Seatwork that fills most of a 50 minute period in the elementary or high school needs to be given in small segments of 5, 10, or 15 minutes. The teacher can check for progress, give more instruction, and have students continue their work. Few students at any grade level are motivated and disciplined enough to work independently and productively for a time span of 40 to 50 minutes. Some students are slow to begin; others complete their work rapidly (some correctly, some incorrectly) and waste time at the end of the period. Other dawdle the entire period without completing the assignment. If long periods of time for independent work are given to students of any age, there is potential for off-task behavior, which leads to misbehavior.

Good and Brophy (1987) suggest that seatwork in reading and language arts activities can be designed to (1) allow students to work successfully and independently, (2) interest students and provide variety in the types of assignments, (3) permit students to read for understanding and pleasure, and (4) occasionally relate to students' personal lives. These suggestions appear to be appropriate criteria for seatwork in any subject area and for any age or grade level. Assigning seatwork that is meaningful, relevant, understandable, and doable is a far more workable approach to securing students' attention than controlling inattention and misbehavior during long periods of seatwork that students see as too difficult and having no relevance to learning.

A list of seatwork assignments suggested by inservice teachers as being potentially challenging, interesting, and contributing to instructional objectives of many classrooms can be found in Form 4.3. These assignments must be adapted to age and achievement level and should be viewed as activities that can interest students if they do not become routine or assigned too frequently. Many of these activities can be used with an entire class and have the potential to increase participation.

Form 4.3 SEATWORK ACTIVITIES THAT HAVE POTENTIAL FOR BEING
INTERESTING, WORTHWHILE, AND CHALLENGING

---

1. *Math*: Give the students five math problems. Two problems should come from a previous lesson and should be easily completed. Two problems should come from the current lesson and have little degree of difficulty. The fifth problem should be more difficult and be marked *Challenge*. Completing the first four problems successfully will give the children a feeling of accomplishment. The fifth problem will give them something to work on.
2. *Language arts*: Provided that the students have had a lesson on poetry, they can be asked to write a poem (haiku, for example). The students should be aware that in an upcoming poetry lesson they will be expected to share their poem, verbally or in writing, with the class.
3. Have students outline a plan for collecting data on a problem in social studies.
4. Have students locate places on an outline map.
5. Have students write a summary of class discussion, the outline for which is written on the board.
6. Have students read in order to answer questions that were placed on the board.
7. Have students draw a cartoon that illustrates an idea.
8. Have students analyze and study cartoons on current events.
9. When studying a phonetic sound, the symbol for the sound is written on the board. Have the pupils read a certain passage and underline all words with that sound.
10. If studying Shakespeare, students could compose headlines and newspaper articles recounting an event in a play. For example, a press release giving an account of Caesar's death could be prepared. As newspaper articles should contain accurate information as to the who, what, when, where, and why of an event, such an assignment would presume that the students have read and are familiar with the play.
11. Given an opening and a closing line, students could compose a short, short story. In a similar vein, students could write a parable if given a moral on which to base their stories.
12. Students could "translate" certain of Shakespeare's soliloquies into today's English language, allowing them to understand more fully the content of the passages.
13. Given the first part of a simile, students could complete the comparisons. For example, "She was as light as a   ."

In order to make seatwork a productive learning experience with maximum student attention and not just a time filler, teachers must have interesting and purposeful seatwork along with a carefully developed plan for assigning and monitoring the work. The following plan for using seatwork was developed and used by special education teachers whose students had demonstrated high levels of time spent on task, achievement, interest, and appropriate behavior.

A Seatwork Plan Developed for Special Education Students

1. Each individual assignment is prepared in advance by the teacher. Because assignments are prepared in this manner, they take into account students' ability to complete the task successfully—usually with a success rate of higher than 80 percent.
2. Because students have difficulty in focusing their attention for prolonged periods of time, seatwork assignments are broken into segments that take students no longer than 10 or 15 minutes to complete.
3. Time between segments (approximately another 10 minutes) is occupied by a "filler task," usually a word or math puzzle. After completion of the filler task the next work segment is begun.
4. On occasion a student can complete all work segments before the end of the work session. The student is then given the choice of going to the reading corner or the listening post or doing another work-related puzzle.
5. One strategy that can be used with individual students is an "ongoing project." The subject of the project is decided by both teacher and student and is intended to take two weeks to complete. The project is used as the filler task between and after completion of work segments.
6. Classroom procedures are highly structured and seldom vary. Students therefore know exactly what they are supposed to be doing at any given time.
7. Monitor and correct seatwork as often as possible. Once students are assured that they are completing tasks successfully, they seem to be enthusiastic about beginning the next one.

Structuring independent seatwork in this manner greatly increases the amount of time students spend "on task." The short, varied work segments reduce the amount of time students spend being unfocused and disruptive. Not only are students more productive when working on assignments, but also the time teachers spend working with individual students is more constructive and seldom compromised by distractions from classmates. In effect, less time is spent maintaining order and more time teaching.

The following rules for seatwork are suggested by experienced teachers.

1. Develop seatwork around the lesson.
2. Present seatwork in the same format as the lesson (i.e., wording, sequence, order of importance).
3. Review assignment before work begins and clear up any confusion such as definitions and directions to underline or circle.
4. Inform students of time limit, ideally less than 10 minutes.
5. Monitor for accuracy.
6. Answer questions to the whole class.
7. Have a positive attitude and voice tone.
8. Solicit questions to draw out the shy ones.
9. Use the same format consistently.
10. Pick the same time each day for seatwork and students will be prepared.

When teachers monitor seatwork activities, what should they watch for or check on? First, look for any students who are not doing the work and give assistance if needed. If no assistance is needed, give a reminder to get to work. This reminder does not always have to be spoken; it may be a smile, a gesture, or a wink, for example. Second, when students are on task, look for accuracy and correctness of work and give assistance if needed. It is important to be quick in giving assistance. Time flies when both student and teacher are academically involved. Before you are aware of the amount of time spent explaining a problem to one student, others may be waiting too long for assistance. Good and Brophy (1987) remind us that when students wait with nothing to do,

> . . . four things can happen and three of them are bad: (1) students may remain interested and attentive; (2) they may become bored or fatigued, losing interest and ability to concentrate; (3) they may become distracted or start daydreaming; or (4) they may actively misbehave. . . . [2]

---

[2]Reprinted from T. Good and J. Brophy, *Looking in Classrooms*, p. 232.

Effective teachers and managers do not monitor only seatwork, they monitor *all* aspects of the classroom environment. Some teachers attempt to teach and are seemingly unaware of student inattention and minor misbehavior. They fail to monitor and act on classroom behavior. Monitoring means keeping a constant check on students' performance and behavior. Teachers should move about the room frequently and give personal attention to students. A quick, quiet conversation such as "Are you having difficulty in getting started?" or "Your beginning sentence is good," or "Remember to capitalize," can have a positive effect on students' effort and attention. Students are more likely to be attentive when the teacher notices both acceptable and unacceptable performance and behavior. Teachers should not only give assistance when students are bogged down, but also they should point out both effective and ineffective learning techniques students are using and, if possible, suggest ways of improving work habits. Remember, classroom observations suggest that the key to higher levels of time spent on task and achievement is the degree to which teachers monitor learning and that the effective monitoring of students' learning significantly reduces the need for disciplinary action (Wyne and Stuck, 1983). Some teacher behaviors associated with effective monitoring have already been discussed in Chapter 3, but because monitoring is so important, the following behaviors are again emphasized.

1. Moving around the classroom.
2. Arranging seating to see all students.
3. Going to the students' desks.
4. Using student assistants for routines.
5. Moving quickly from student to student.
6. When working with one student, be aware of the entire classroom.
7. Monitoring for performance and behavior.

PACING

Pacing refers to the amount of time allotted to an activity or objective. You probably already know that the amount of content covered can significantly affect student achievement. Barr's (1980) well-known study of reading achievement showed that 80 percent of differences in reading achievement was due to the pace of instruction. Other studies have confirmed that covering curriculum at a brisk pace increases achievement (Good, Grouws, and Beckerman, 1978).

Some teachers feel they cannot move on until all students have mastered a topic or skill; however, in heterogeneous classes a lesson that is ideally paced for the slowest students will not be ideally paced for the fastest learners. Obviously, content coverage has to be reasonably well paced for all students.

Effective classroom managers pace instruction to maximize students' attention.

Teachers need to observe students' work and make frequent checks to determine if they are performing at a satisfactory level. If students' work shows a large number have mastered the skill and content, quicken the pace; if large numbers fail to perform at an acceptable level, slow the pace. One or two students who are far ahead or far below most student's level of achievement may need individual assistance. Students who are bored because there is too little work or frustrated because there is too much become problem children. An appropriate instructional pace will help maximize student attention and contribute to appropriate behavior.

One other comment about pacing. Keep the lesson moving by avoiding dwelling too long on one point, talking, preaching, or nagging that is obviously beyond what is necessary for most students. Dwelling too long on one point impedes the momentum of the lesson and can allow and encourage student inattention and misbehavior.

UTILIZING FEEDBACK

Teachers who keep students actively engaged in learning provide verbal and nonverbal feedback about performance and behaviors. Feedback should take into account the age and nature of the learner. Young students may need more frequent feedback than older students.

Effective classroom managers give feedback that motivates and maximizes students' attention.

Remember, one of the requisites for effective classroom management discussed in Chapter 2 is that teachers must respect students. If teachers respect students, the feedback they give students will reflect that respect. Teachers who respect students will avoid sarcasm and criticism of the student as a person. Feedback that makes students uncomfortable, defensive, and feel like nobodies distracts their attention and creates conditions that encourage inappropriate behavior.

Dr. Haim Ginott's (1972) example of a verbal exchange between a teacher and a nine-year-old child is a classic illustration of a teacher's lack of respect, attacking the student as a person.

> Felix, age nine, complained to his teacher that a boy from the sixth grade had hit him over the head with a book.
>
> TEACHER: He just came over and hit you! Just like that! You didn't do anything. You were just an innocent bystander, and he was a perfect stranger.
>
> FELIX: (in tears) Yes.
>
> TEACHER: I don't believe you. You must have done something. I know you. When it comes to provoking, you are an expert.
>
> FELIX: I didn't do anything. I just stood in the hall, minding my own business.
>
> TEACHER: I'm in the hall every day. No one ever attacks me. How come you always attract trouble? You'd better watch out of one of these days you'll be in very hot water.
>
> Felix put his head on the desk and cried while his teacher turned to the business of the day.[3]

Ginott suggests that instead of using destructive feedback, this teacher could have mirrored the student's feelings with feedback such as: "It must have hurt awfully." "You must have felt furious." "It must have made you angry." "Write up the whole incident for me, if you want to, and I'll see what I can do about it."

Sensitive teachers try to avoid making demands. Demands only increase defiance. Children hate to be ordered around. Wise teachers know cooperation is better than force. They avoid harsh commands such as, "Do what you are told!" They say, "Remember what we are supposed to do?" Instead of giving commands, they take a "kinder, gentler" approach that allows students to decide an appropriate course of action. For example, they might say, "Your pencil is on the floor,"

---

[3]Reprinted from H. Ginott, *Teacher and Child*, p. 63.

instead of "Pick up your pencil;" or "The assignment is on page 89," instead of "Open your book to page 89;" or "I can't hear for the noise," instead of "Stop that noise." Statements such as these illustrate differences in feedback which affect levels of cooperation, resistance, and defiance. Feedback informs students as to how others view them. It tells them that both appropriate and inappropriate behavior is recognized. It can encourage and correct and teach discipline. In order to be helpful feedback must have certain characteristics. First, it should be descriptive, not evaluative. For example, "That was a stupid thing to do," is evaluative, and "Your behavior is preventing you and your neighbor from learning," is descriptive. Second, feedback is based on the needs of both the giver and the receiver. Feedback that serves only the needs of the giver can be destructive to the receiver. When teachers who want to help students perceive that students need to change their behavior, then the feedback must be informative, not simply reflect the frustration of the teacher. Helpful feedback must also be directed toward behavior that the student can do something about. Comments and behavior that remind students of situations about which they have no control tend to increase inappropriate behavior. For example, snide comments about tardiness caused by parents' schedules only serve to embarrass the student or create hostility. Third, feedback should be clearly and correctly understood by the receiver. It is often a good idea to have the student rephrase the feedback to see if the student's perception parallels what the teacher intended. The nature and age of the learner should also be kept in mind. Young students may need feedback more often than older ones do. Finally, helpful feedback is specific rather than general. A comment such as, "You can write a better paper" gives no help. A better comment might be, "You may want to take a look at the rule for a good topic sentence." Effective teachers use appropriate feedback to help students with learning tasks; they avoid feedback that criticizes and impedes learning. More will be said about avoiding criticism in Chapter 6.

Form 4.4 CHARACTERISTICS OF EFFECTIVE FEEDBACK

1. Feedback should be descriptive.
2. Feedback should serve the needs of the teacher and the student.
3. Feedback is addressed to behavior the student is able to do something about.

4. Feedback must be clearly and correctly understood by the receiver.
5. Effective feedback is specific.

Write an example of teacher feedback which illustrates these five fundamentals of effective feedback.

Form 4.5 FEEDBACK TO A TOTAL CLASS WHICH HELPS GET AND HOLD STUDENTS' ATTENTION

Comments made enthusiastically but naturally (not stilted or forced) while teaching:

1. Let's see who knows. Raise your hands.
2. I know you will do your best.
3. I'm glad you asked and that you raised your hand to find out what we are doing.
4. We need everyone's eyes on the board.
5. This is a matter of working at it.
6. I see a lot of you know what we are doing.
7. I want to see who will come to the board. Raise your hand.
8. If you have been doing nice work, you may show it to me or another person.
9. Now, you think about this.
10. I'll put a hint on the board.
11. You see! You already know what to do.

SECURING PARTICIPATION

Many teachers tend to call on students whom they believe are better students more frequently than they call on students whom they believe are less capable. Students who participate in class are more likely to get feedback and encouragement that enhances their chances for success than do children who do not participate. In a classroom of 25 to 35 students it is often easy to overlook students who do not actively volunteer to participate in discussions and other teacher-student and student-student interactions. We should take mental inventory at the end of the day or class period to ascertain which students have not actively participated. Plan to "force" these students to participate the next day or next period. Make a mental or written note to call on those students, and plan to create a situation that will ensure their successful participation.

> Effective classroom managers encourage student participation.

Instruction usually takes place in groups; the larger the group, the less opportunity each student has to participate. Therefore, we need to find methods that allow all or many students to participate at the same time instead of one student at a time. For example, a common practice in many classrooms is to ask one to five students to go to the board and solve a problem or other exercise. The remainder of the class is told, "Pay attention to the work on the board. You may be asked a question about it." While the one student (or more) is working at the board, other students give little or no attention because their only task is to watch. In typical classrooms many students do not watch, loud talking and inappropriate behavior erupt, and the teacher has to quiet down the group before the student at the board can explain his or her work. Frequently, few if any students listen to the explanation.

This scenario can be changed by asking all students in the instructional group to solve the problem or do the activity at their seats. The teacher can walk around the classroom and monitor for attention to task and correctness. Students who need help are given that help quickly and efficiently. All students are attending to learning. And remember, as always, when students' attention is on learning, they are less likely to be disruptive. Form 4.6 is a list of suggestions made by experienced teachers for increasing and encouraging students' participation and therefore, maximizing students' attention to task.

Form 4.6 WAYS TO INCREASE STUDENT PARTICIPATION

1. Give opinion questions in all areas of study and activities. Let each student know his or her opinion is worthy of being heard.
2. Use "bribery." Offer rewards for exceptional performance or high quality of response. For example, some teachers use everything from "free time," to extra credit grades, to discount movie tickets.
3. Assign activities that every student must do; for example, stand and face north, or locate your address on a map.
4. Assign each student information to bring to class on a specific day of the week; for example, students A–D bring information on Monday, E–K on Tuesday, and so on.
5. Have students put thumbs up if a statement is correct, thumbs down if incorrect.
6. Have students practice a drill in unison, (e.g., foreign language drills).
7. Divide students into teams and have a contest.

8. Allow for enough "wait time" after asking a question. This gives students time to formulate an answer.
9. Have students role play environmental and social issues or historical events. Assign each student a role, and have students act their roles as depicted in their reading.
10. Put a question or problem on the board. Have all students answer or solve the problem at their desks. Then call on one student to respond.
11. Divide the class into teams and give each team a project. Each team member is then given the responsibility for a part of the project.
12. Assign peer coaches. Helping others is a way of participating.
13. When teaching word problems in math, read the problem and have all students raise one finger if you add to solve the problem, two fingers if you subtract, three if you multiply, four fingers if you divide.
14. When studying adjectives and adverbs, read or have students read a sentence. Indicate the word under analysis and have students raise one finger if it is an adjective, two fingers if it is an adverb.
15. The study of nouns and pronouns, common nouns and proper nouns, metaphors and similes, and so on can be handled in the same manner.

SUMMARY

In Chapter 4 you have learned that maximizing students' attention and participation minimizes inappropriate behavior. Specifically, you have learned that in order to maximize attention you need to (1) get and hold students' attention, (2) use time for learning efficiently and effectively, (3) hold realistic expectations for students, (4) monitor independent work that is at the appropriate achievement level of the students, (5) pace instruction in relation to students' ability to "keep up," (6) give feedback that increases attention to task, (7) secure active participation of all students, and (8) make plans to resolve behavior problems. (See Form 4.7.)

Form 4.7 CHECKLIST FOR EVALUATING STUDENTS' ATTENTION TO LEARNING

How did you maximize students' attention?

1. By having a well-planned, interesting lesson.
2. By having materials ready to use.
3. By efficient handling of materials.
4. By using a variety of teaching techniques.
5. By working for wide student participation.

6. By giving individualized and interesting assignments appropriate for each student's level of achievement and behavior.
7. By using chalkboard, maps, and other teaching materials.
8. By monitoring student work for understanding and performance.
9. By pacing instruction in relation to students' ability to "keep up."
10. By giving interesting seatwork.
11. By giving feedback that gets and holds students' attention.
12. Other.

In this chapter we have discussed only a few aspects of teaching and learning which are used by effective teachers to maximize students' attention to learning. It is assumed that you have already learned or will learn a myriad of teaching methods that will work well for you; however, some additional teacher behaviors which affect students' attention will be discussed in Chapter 5.

Form 4.8 GUIDES FOR GETTING AND HOLDING STUDENTS' ATTENTION

1. Get the attention of each member of the class before plunging into the lesson.
2. Generally speaking, explain a correction of one or more student errors to the whole class. Others may be making the same mistake.
3. Involve students in explaining and answering questions instead of assuming total responsibility for all that goes on in the class.
4. Speak in an authoritative tone that gives the impression that something important is going on.
5. Keep to the lesson; don't get drawn off the purpose of the lesson.
6. Use language students understand.
7. Check to see that essential concepts have been learned.
8. Ask clear, concise questions.
9. Teach in such a manner that students must prepare for class and cannot depend on the teacher for the content. This diminishes student interest.
10. Give specific and appropriate feedback to student's comments.
11. Pace instruction and speech so that students understand.
12. Ask a question before calling on a particular student to answer.
13. Monitor seatwork for correctness and understanding.
14. Make assignments that are worthwhile.
15. Hold students accountable for assignments.
16. Check *all* assignments.
17. Use adult speech when you are instructing; "baby talk" fosters immature behavior.
18. Give clear directions. Ask students to repeat or put directions in their own words.
19. Expect good things from students.
20. Plan for specifics and the generalizations you will teach in the academic and behavior areas.

Remember, to be an effective classroom manager the teacher must (1) have respect of students; (2) be consistent, and therefore, credible and dependable; (3) assume responsibility for students' learning; (4) value and enjoy learning; and (5) communicate and model these attitudes. These attitudes are requisite to effective management and may be more important to maximizing student attention and participation than any other aspect of management and teaching. If you model these attitudes, you will have maximized your own attention to the teaching task.

In Part Two you have seen the importance of preventing management and discipline problems. Part Three is devoted to resolving behavior problems, teaching discipline, and maintaining an effectively managed classroom.

QUESTIONS AND ACTIVITIES

4.1 Arrange to visit the classroom of a teacher who is well organized. Notice how that teacher deals with routine procedures. Keep a time log that tells how each minute in the class period was spent. Look for and record transition time from activity to activity.

4.2 If you are teaching, try voice variations as you interact with your class. Speak loudly and softly; quicken and slow your speech. How do students react?

4.3 Plan an "attention getting" lesson beginning. Why do you think it will work? If possible, teach the lesson beginning to a class or a group of your peers.

4.4 Review the plan for getting students' attention made by the beginning secondary teacher. Make one of your own to solve a common problem of inattention such as talking to one's neighbor.

4.5 Do you think problems of inattention are different in elementary and secondary schools? Explain your answer.

4.6 Make a list of ways you can get students' attention.

4.7 Describe a classroom in which time is used efficiently.

4.8 List teacher behaviors that demonstrate effective use of time.

4.9 Plan a lesson in any subject area; then design appropriate seatwork activities to enhance this lesson. Seatwork may be for practice, remediation, or extension of learning.

4.10 If you are student teaching, observe a lesson taught by your directing teacher and use what you know about pacing to determine if the pace is appropriate. If you are not teaching, observe one of your college classes to determine if it is appropriately paced.

4.11 Observe a teacher and record the teacher's feedback to students. See if you can devise other appropriate responses to the same behavior.

4.12 Observe a teacher and listen to tone of voice the teacher uses to deliver feedback. What does the tone say?

4.13 List ways you can encourage students to participate.

4.14 List ways you can "force" all students to participate.

4.15 Describe the behavior of one of your former teachers who was able to keep students on task.

4.16 Plan and teach a lesson that meets the criteria for an appropriate, interesting, and challenging lesson.

4.17 List reasons why a good lesson, skillfully executed, prevents misbehavior.

4.18 Add to the list of ways to maximize student attention in Form 4.8.

4.19 Observe a lesson, or have someone observe you teach. Make a list of ways you or the teacher maximized students' attention. Begin with the following items:

    (a) By a well planned lesson.

    (b) Having materials ready for immediate use.

    (c) Having an interesting beginning.

    (d) By varying activities.

    (e) By having wide participation.

    (f) By differentiated assignments to meet varying achievement levels.

    (g) By monitoring.

    If you skillfully executed a well-planned lesson, you might use techniques not covered in this chapter.

4.20 Plan the most interesting lesson you possibly can. Then ask, "What can I do to make this lesson even more interesting?"

REFERENCES

Anderson, L., Brubaker, N., Alleman-Brooks, J., and Duffy, G. (1985). "A Qualitative Study of Seatwork in First Grade Classrooms." *Elementary School Journal*, 86, pp. 123–140.

Barr, R. (1980). *School, Class, Group and Pace Effects on Learning*. Paper presented at the annual meeting of the American Educational Research Association, Boston, Mass.

Berliner, D. (1984). "The Half-Full Glass: A Review of Research on Teaching." In P. L. Hosford (ed.) *Using What We Know About Teaching*. Alexandria,

Va.: Association for Supervision and Curriculum Development, pp. 51–56.

Brophy, J. (1987). "Synthesis of Research on Strategies for Motivating Students to Learn." *Educational Leadership, 45* (2), pp. 40–48.

Brophy, J., and Good, T. (1974). *Teacher-Student Relationships: Causes and Consequences.* New York: Holt, Rinehart, and Winston.

Bureau of Staff Development (1986–87). *Classroom Management.* Miami, Fla.: Dade County Public Schools. Appendix I, pp. 9–11.

Ginott, H. (1972). *Teacher and Child.* Toronto: Macmillan, pp. 63–64.

Good, T., and Brophy, J. (1987). *Looking in Classrooms* (4th ed.). New York: Harper and Row, pp. 247, 232.

Good, T., Grouws, D., and Beckerman, T. (1978). "Curriculum Pacing: Some Empirical Data in Mathematics." *Journal of Curriculum Studies, 10,* pp. 75–81.

Goodlad, J. (1984). *A Place Called School.* New York: McGraw-Hill.

Institute for Research on Teaching (Summer, 1984). "Seatwork Can Be More Productive." *Communication Quarterly, 7* (1), p. 4.

Kounin, J. (1970). *Discipline and Group Management in Classrooms.* New York: Holt, Rinehart, and Winston.

Porter, A., and Brophy, J. (1988). "Synthesis of Research and Good Teaching: Insights from the Work of the Institute for Research on Teaching. *Educational Leadership, 45* (8), pp. 74–85.

Stallings, J. (1980). "Allocated Academic Learning Time Revisited, or Beyond Time on Task." *Educational Researcher, 9,* pp. 11–16.

Wyne, M., and Stuck, G. (1983). "Time and Learning: Implications for the Classroom Teacher." *Elementary School Journal, 83* (1), pp. 67–74, 70–71.

PART
Three

RESOLVING PROBLEMS AND MAINTAINING AN EFFECTIVELY MANAGED CLASSROOM

*W*hen teachers communicate and model behaviors that indicate they respect students, value and enjoy learning, assume responsibility for learning, are credible and dependable, and maximize students' attention to learning, many behavior problems can be prevented and self-discipline can be learned. Once these essential attitudes are communicated and conditions for successful management and displaying self-discipline are created, there still remains the task of maintaining and nurturing this environment.

Student behavior in any classroom can be unpredictable and mercurial. Students' needs to socialize, exert influence, establish their identities, and grow up predictably and frequently lead to some form of behavior that needs attention. Even though every effort is made to prevent inappropriate behavior, it may still occur in varying degrees of unacceptability. In Chapter 5 strategies for resolving management and discipline problems that occur in many classrooms in varying degrees are suggested. Chapter 6 is devoted to teaching discipline and maintaining an effectively managed classroom.

Chapter
5

Resolving Problems: General Strategies

INTRODUCTION AND OBJECTIVES

Throughout this book the emphasis has been on creating conditions that prevent inappropriate behavior and foster appropriate conduct and self-discipline. However, "children will be children," and in most classrooms students will at least occasionally misbehave. Even in well-managed classrooms where teachers model expectations and foster self-discipline, minor and major problems can arise with individual students and even the entire classroom group; however, a prevalence of discipline problems indicates deficiencies in the classroom climate or in management strategies. The first action of teachers with discipline and management problems should be to assess their own attitudes, behavior, expectations, instruction, and the general climate. Remember, many teachers attribute misconduct to the nature of their students and fail to look at their own behavior and at the nature of the classroom climate. The focus of this chapter is resolving management and discipline problems, but the reader should also be mindful that the principles already given for preventing problems and teaching self-discipline when applied consistently are also fundamental to resolving both major and minor behavior problems.

It is difficult to classify many behavior problems as major or minor, because almost all minor problems have the potential for becoming major problems if they are not resolved. Perhaps the reason some teachers over-react to minor incidents is that they know the potential of misbehavior to spread and become more frequent and intense. For example, the inappropriate behavior of one student that spreads to several others is a major problem. If one student "talks out," the business of teaching and learning can still be carried on; but if many students "talk out," teaching and learning are sacrificed. If one student is occasionally disrespectful of the teacher and other students, the classroom climate may not be shattered and teaching and learning can go on; but if that student is continuously disrespectful, or if many students are disrespectful of each other and the teacher, little constructive teaching and learning can occur. A problem may be classified as a major one when it destroys even one student's ability to attend to learning and requires constant and concentrated teacher attention.

The following list of behavior problems that arise in classrooms was compiled by beginning teachers. Which ones would you classify as minor and under what conditions? Can you add to the list?

rowdiness, horseplay	smoking
setting fires and smoke	tardiness
disturbance	fighting
rudeness, poor manners	truancy
writing on walls	ethnic conflicts
showing off	stealing
running and pushing in	tattling
halls and classrooms	teasing
careless with materials	carrying grudges
and equipment	getting even
carrying and showing	carrying knives or other
obscene literature	weapons
cliques	failing to follow
cheating	directions
drug abuse	doing nothing
nuisance actions	talking
swearing	name-calling
"taking up" for friends	getting out of seats
failing to do work	

Unfortunately, many of these problems can be found to some degree in many classrooms. Some teachers try to ignore problems and attempt to teach, but effective classroom teachers believe they can help students resolve these behaviors, and they act on that belief. Researchers Brophy and Rohrkemper (1981) found that ineffective teachers often rely on threats or punishment to control misbehavior when it occurs, whereas effective teachers use long-term approaches intended to solve the problems, not merely stop the behavior. Helping students resolve behavior problems takes time, effort, and intense, consistent use of principles of effective management and discipline. Resolving problems can be as subtle as a mild desist or as drastic as expulsion. In this chapter some of the principles of management and discipline already discussed as ways of preventing problems are reviewed and extended as ways of resolving problems; other principles are also introduced.

After completing this chapter the preservice and beginning teacher will be able to

- recognize and understand the difference between minor problems and major problems,
- utilize mild desists to resolve problems,
- recognize the need to change the learning environment,
- suggest ways to change the learning environment to increase appropriate behavior,
- recognize the importance of involving students in problem solving,
- apply the six steps in the scientific process of problem solving to resolving student behavior problems,
- help students define a behavior problem,
- conduct brainstorming sessions to arrive at possible solutions to problem behavior,
- write a contract for resolving a behavior problem,
- list some behaviors that could be changed by using some principles of behavior modification,
- list some of the objections many teachers have to behavior modification,
- suggest appropriate socialization strategies to resolve specific behavior problems,
- recognize problem behavior that may have to be stopped by punitive disciplinary measures,
- suggest alternatives to harsh punishment, and
- use guidelines for effectively administering disciplinary measures.

UTILIZING MILD DESISTS

Teacher monitoring and desisting behaviors have already been discussed as methods of preventing inappropriate behavior and practicing self-discipline; however, desists can also be used to resolve minor problems that arise in many classrooms. When used, they should be unobtrusive, quiet reminders or suggestions for alternative behavior (Kounin, 1970). Desists are most effective if the teacher is not upset or angry and does not make a mountain of a molehill.

> Effective classroom managers use desists to stop and resolve inappropriate behavior.

Although many behavior problems can be prevented, minor misbehavior will sometimes occur and recur, because self-discipline is not acquired in a day, a week, a month, or even a year. Many, if not most, minor problems can be resolved by using a few simple, unobtrusive desisting procedures that take little time and energy. The following desisting procedures used by experienced teachers are often effective in getting students to stop and think and therefore resolve their own behavior problems:

1. Make eye contact with student, and look the student clearly in the eye.
2. Move closer to the student.
3. Place finger to lips to indicate "stop talking."
4. Shake or nod head.
5. Point to student; say nothing.
6. Restate a rule.
7. Have student state a rule and follow the rule.
8. Frown or smile at student(s).
9. Turn lights lower or brighter to gain attention.
10. Stop your activity for a moment and be silent.

If teachers are keenly observant and immediately utilize mild desists to remind students of inappropriate behavior, most students will respond appropriately; however, many minor problems often develop into major ones. Talking when others are talking; shouting, yelling, and not paying attention; getting out of seats; annoying others; and not following directions occur in most classrooms. If these ordinarily mundane behaviors are not stopped when only one or a few students are involved, they will destroy the learning environment and the teacher's authority. When only a few students display these behaviors, mild desists can be effective. If the entire class is involved, then teachers should recognize that other strategies must be used. They should also recognize that if desisting procedures are to be effective, they must be used when the problem behavior first occurs and when only one or two students are involved. Some teachers tend to ignore misbehavior until it becomes widespread and too late for using quick, decisive, and effective desists.

Some descriptions and analyses of their discipline and management problems by student teachers illustrate their failure to recognize the potential effectiveness of desists; however, they did recognize that making mountains of molehills is counterproductive.

Student 1

One of my biggest problems is discipline. Since I teach kindergarten, I think one of the major reasons for my discipline problem is due to the short attention span of the children. When I begin a lesson, most of the children are listening, but in ten minutes, I usually "lose" some of the children. No matter how much I involve them, some of the children cannot listen for more than approximately ten minutes. Even if I do a variety of activities during a lesson—for example, finger plays, songs, follow-me games—some of the children are still not able to continue with the lesson.

Another big problem of mine is that I call attention to anyone who isn't listening to me, who is talking and who isn't sitting the way he should, etc. In other words, I stop whatever I'm doing and tell a child to stop his misbehavior. As a result, I "lose" a few other children in an attempt to bring back one. I guess I have to learn to overlook some misbehavior, as long as it doesn't distract too many others.

Obviously, this teacher needs to use unobtrusive, mild desists, not overlook the behavior. Perhaps ignoring the behavior in the past is what led to this teacher's minor problems becoming major problems. Ignoring behavior does not diminish or extinguish it; ignoring usually leads to an increase in that behavior. Generally speaking, a rule of thumb is when you would like to ignore behavior, try mild desists. Note that this teacher is blaming the nature of the students, and not the environment, for their behavior. A change in teaching methods and procedures may be necessary in addition to desisting behaviors in order to change the classroom climate.

Student 2

I attribute my discipline problems to many factors. First, the children are young and their attention span limited. If I see they are not getting what I am trying to teach, I push harder, thinking they will learn. The more I push, the more restless they get; and thus I get upset. I become angry at myself because I feel that I have failed. Sometimes I expect too much from these children, not realizing that they do not know some things that I do because they have not been around as long. The major reason I feel I have problems is that I do not overlook some of the children's actions. If a child is restless, I will stop the class, make a comment and "lose" about ten others while I am doing it. Each time I stop I get upset, and then I sometimes take it out on the children. If I realize these children are tiny and have only been around for five years and have a bit more patience, I would overlook much more and my discipline would not be so extreme.

Notice that this teacher feels if she "overlooked" discipline problems, they would go away. A change in teaching content, methods, and expectations might be needed. Notice that both teachers realize that when they make an effort to stop misbehavior by calling it to the students' attention and reprimanding (probably threatening), the disruptive behavior spreads and other students lose self control. This "ripple effect" is a common occurrence when discipline measures are ineffective. Notice that student 3 recognizes that the teacher is responsible for the "ripple effect."

Student 3

We have some pretty bad discipline problems. My directing teacher has the children write notes to their parents telling them what they did that was wrong. This works out well in some cases. However, I feel that she spends too much time picking at details which I would ignore, such as shirt tails hanging out and combs in hair. Also, she draws attention to trouble-makers and seems to reinforce their trouble-making.

When desisting behaviors fail to resolve problems, then teachers must use more direct and assertive behavior to intervene in more visible and forceful ways. One common and often effective intervention strategy is to change the classroom environment.

CHANGING THE ENVIRONMENT

Certain aspects of the classroom environment may be desirable in one learning situation and prove detrimental to learning in other situations. Effective teachers and managers are quick to recognize that changes in the classroom can be effective in resolving behavior problems.

> Effective classroom managers resolve problems by changing the learning environment.

Effective classroom managers use nonpunitive intervention techniques such as immediate change or restructuring of a classroom activity, providing immediate help to one or all students, boosting interest of one or all students, providing more structure for one or all students, and using humor. For example, an entire class is restless, anxious, and calling out answers in a circuslike atmosphere. A teacher can immediately resort to quiet participation activities by having students raise one finger if the math problem should be solved by adding, two fingers by subtracting, three fingers if it requires multiplication, and so on. Oral answers are not acceptable.

If the group appears bored and inattentive, ask for opinions, focus on student interest, or make the topic or task relevant to students' needs or interests. When one student or a small group of students does not understand and is misbehaving, provide immediate, practical, tangible help for these students. If the classroom is really tense and students' behavior is on the verge of bedlam, make a joke, relieve the tension, and begin something interesting.

An intervention may be as simple as saying, "Stop whatever you are doing. Sit, be quiet, and listen for one minute," or "Stop! Think about this question. I will ask each of you for an answer," or "Stop. Write the answer to this question. You have three minutes." You may also ask, "What is the problem?" In many instances honest communication between teacher and students will reveal reasons for problems and suggest solutions. A class may tell the teacher about an incident before school or on the playground which caused the excitement. A teacher who has good rapport with students is likely to receive honest, valid information from them about their behavior and can then proceed to make needed adjustments in the environment and help students make behavior changes that resolve problems.

One student teacher solved the problem of a "class clown" by

> . . . having him be the teacher during a math lesson. He saw very quickly that it was not easy to stand in front of the class and keep everyone in line. Since then, he has been very well behaved and even tries to help me keep order.

When teachers have a profusion of behavior problems, they can change the environment by making aspects that contribute to problems less attractive, or they can simplify and restrict the environment. One of the most common changes that simplifies and restricts is removing a student from the classroom or from an area of the classroom. This procedure is referred to as "time out." "Time out" can be as simple as having a student move away from other students and remain in the new area until the student feels she or he can return to the original position and not disrupt the activity of other students. "Time out" can also involve consequences or conditions that must be met before the student returns to the classroom or to his or her original seating. The consequences can be such things as completion of work, writing essays on how to behave, no social contact with peers, or a conference with a school administrator.

Form 5.1 CHANGING THE LEARNING ENVIRONMENT TO RESOLVE PROBLEMS

1. Add magazines, games, and so on when students need stimulation to learn.
2. Remove magazines, games, and so on when they distract students' attention from learning tasks.
3. Create special interest or fun areas.
4. Declare special interest and fun areas off limits at certain times and under certain conditions.
5. Prepare durable materials that allow students to use them without constant monitoring.
6. Arrange seating with students' individual behavior and academic and social needs in mind.
7. Move a student from one area of the classroom to another or out of the classroom altogether.
8. Place a student behind the chalkboard or other barrier that "isolates" the student.
9. Change activities from passive to active or from active to passive.
10. When possible give students a choice of activities.

The preceding suggestions for using desists and changing the environment often work to eliminate surface misconduct, but they are usually the answer neither to coping with students' serious emotional problems nor to problems such as lack of student motivation, academic achievement, and self-discipline. The latter are indicative of fundamental deficiencies in the classroom situation. Their resolution generally has to be long-term and must involve students.

UTILIZING PROBLEM SOLVING

Research findings on how teachers resolve behavior problems indicate that teachers judged most effective in dealing with problems are more likely to involve students in changing their behavior and resolving problems than are teachers judged to be less effective managers (Brophy and Rohrkemper, 1981). Effective managers also use long-term, solution-oriented approaches to solving behavior problems and punish students less than other teachers. Ineffective managers often rely on threats or punishment, are less verbal, appear more distant from students, and use fewer supportive behaviors and problem-solving approaches than do effective managers (Brophy and Rohrkemper, 1980).

> Effective classroom managers use problem-solving techniques to resolve misbehavior.

A simple approach to a complex process is to help students stop and think about what they have done or are about to do. Many students respond to situations without thinking. They can be taught to analyze, ignore provocations, and to resolve problems instead of responding to problems in an impetuous manner.

Students are involved in solving behavior problems when teachers make statements or ask questions that allow or require students to think about their behavior and remind them of their values and what is important to them. Statements such as the following give students information to think about and they imply that students have a choice in how they behave:

1. If you continue to use time by talking, there will be no time left to plan our party, field trip, and so on.
2. If you continue to treat your classmates in this way, how do you expect them to feel about you?
3. Do you understand the consequences of your conduct?
4. I cannot permit you to act in this way and continue to be your teacher.

Students must choose to behave appropriately or inappropriately, and they must be made aware of and accept the consequences of their behavior. Teachers, in turn, must be prepared to assist in helping students to arrive at alternative ways of behaving and give students the opportunity to prove they are capable of making choices and solving their own problems.

Many teachers are able to get students to try to resolve problems through private conferencing, which enables students to reflect on their behavior in a supportive atmosphere. Some teachers even give students training in problem solving.

Some suggestions for conferencing with students who have behavior problems such as temper tantrums, arguing, quickness to anger, calling others names, self-appointed monitors follow. Remember, all dialogue must be carried on in a supportive, noncritical manner.

1. Remind students they can change the behavior. Use positive statements such as, "I know you can refrain from calling others names."
2. Remind students they are not responsible for the behavior of others.
3. Let students know that losing an argument is alright.
4. Help students recognize when and if anger, jealousy, arguing, and so on are worth the effort.
5. Help students to recognize how others feel and to face their own feelings.

Some problem behaviors that may be resolved by conferencing with the student privately are tattling, cheating, lying, defensive behavior, failure to complete work, and picking on others. We must keep in mind however, that we are not counselors, psychologists, or psychiatrists and that some behaviors are manifestations of deeply rooted psychological problems requiring professional counseling.

None of the preceding suggestions is easily carried out, but each is worth a try. If the students respect you and know you are dependable and credible, they may listen and learn from some of the insights you can share with them. They are looking for help but may initially resist your efforts to help them clarify their problems and change this behavior. Remember that not all students will respond to questioning and conferencing in a positive manner. Involving students in resolving behavior problems requires effort, patience, time, and skill. Many educators believe, and research findings support the view, that the results are worth the time and effort. Methods such as conferencing will be effective with some students, but a more comprehensive approach to problems will be needed for many students.

The comprehensive approach to problem solving most often advocated by experts in all fields of inquiry is the "scientific method." Thomas Gordon (1974) says that teachers can utilize the six steps in the scientific method to solve behavior and management problems as easily and effectively as scientists in other fields use the process. You are probably already familiar with the six steps and need only apply them to resolving students' behavior problems. The steps of the scientific method are as follows:

1. Define the problem clearly, accurately, and to the satisfaction of all persons involved. Students should willingly enter into the process and understand that this is not a phony way of conning them into changing behavior. The teacher should have as much information as possible about the problem and the student or students. The teacher should find a time to confer with the student when there will be no interruptions. Tell the student there is a problem that must be solved, and emphasize that you want to find a way to work through this problem. Looking beyond the behavior and getting past it to identify the real problem is often a part of this step.

2. Brainstorm as many solutions as possible. Make no judgment about any proposed solution at this point. Keep all ideas before the student or group. Write down all suggestions, and insist on additional alternatives until it appears there are no more.

3. Evaluate the suggested solutions. Begin by eliminating those that are obviously unacceptable to the teacher or the student. Judge each alternative on the basis of how well it meets the needs of all persons involved, its effect on others, and the probability of its being a lasting solution. At this point it may be possible to combine two or more alternatives to create a better

one. The student or group and the teacher should give reasons why an alternative has merit. It is often a good idea to have persons advocating a certain alternative make a list of its positives and negatives.

4. Decide on the best solution by consensus of the group and the teacher or by mutual agreement between the teacher and the student or group. Do not vote; this may result in students being poorly motivated to accept the decision and solve the problem. Put the solution in writing. At this point you have a written agreement between teacher and student; you may want to sign and have the student sign this agreement, or you may simply want to have an oral commitment. Whatever procedure is used, be sure there is a valid agreement and that students are not grudgingly submitting to something they really do not like.

5. Make plans to implement the decision. Make sure everyone knows and understands responsibilities. Failure to decide who will do something and when and how it is to be done will result in failure to solve the problem. Finally, write a plan for implementing the decision and give it to the student or group of students.

6. Evaluate the success of the plan. Discuss progress or lack of progress in resolving the problem with the student or group. Not all decisions and implementation plans turn out to be good ones. A poor solution may have been chosen, and a new or modified solution and plan may have to be found. If a new approach to the problem is tried, involve students in making that decision and its implementation.

Problems are not resolved by ordering, demanding, and threatening; neither are they resolved because the teacher has a solution. They are resolved when a solution is found that is acceptable to both students and teacher. The six-step scientific method is an excellent way to find that solution. For example, a junior high school teacher used the scientific process to resolve a major behavior problem in the following way. Note the process and the students' input.

Students in Ms. Y's seventh grade, basic math course used obscene language when they talked with their peers and the teacher. If the teacher left the classroom, turned her back, or answered the door, a shower of paper airplanes with obscene words inundated her desk and the area in front of the chalkboard. Ms. Y's class was generally passive and apathetic except for the obscene language; however, few if any students did homework or seatwork. After six weeks of this behavior, Ms. Y decided to lecture students on their behavior, tear up obscene papers, and assign more work, which was never done. Ms. Y thought she had good rapport with the students, for they never attacked her personally; but when she thought about her relationship with this class, she realized that she never really talked "with" these students. She always talked "to" them. She decided to talk "with" them about this problem.

When the students arrived and were seated, she said in as gentle a tone as possible, "Class, I am disturbed about the obscene language which is written and spoken in this room. This is a real problem for me. Can you help me understand why this type of language is used so often?" There was a period of silence, and no one moved. Ms. Y continued, "Can you tell me why you are doing this? Is it that you think it is cute or funny or smart?" Silence again. She continued, "I want to solve this problem for your benefit and mine. What is causing you to behave this way? It interferes with your learning and my teaching. Let's talk."

Finally, a student she thought was rather shy said, "We are angry." "Why are you angry?" Several students spoke at once, "Because we don't understand how to do the work in this class."

Ms. Y was surprised. She assumed these students were capable of doing the work and were simply unmotivated. "What don't you understand?" A flood of anger- and resentment-filled comments poured out. Ms. Y was stunned. She said, "What can we do to resolve this? I hear you, and I will see what I can do to make the work easier and more relevant; but tell me exactly what you want."

She asked a student to go to the board and write suggestions. Ideas such as repeat directions three times, no homework, thorough instruction to be given before homework assignments were made, and cover no more than three pages in the text per week were listed.

Ms. Y looked over the list and told the class she could agree to some of these suggestions, but not to others. After a lively discussion, the class and Ms. Y came up with a list of things which Ms. Y could do. She then asked for a list of suggestions for students' behavior. One of the first was no more obscenity; other suggestions were listen in class, complete homework and seatwork if they could do it.

Ms. Y listed the suggestions for student action, which all students agreed to try. She informed the students she would write the list of things for the teachers to do and a list of things for students to do and give each student a copy. Each student would sign Ms. Y's copy, and she in turn would sign each student's copy. The class agreed to try the suggestions for a period of two weeks.

A list of consequences for failure to implement suggestions was also drawn up by the class. Two of the most interesting were (1) if a student used obscene language, that student would receive double homework assignments for one week, and (2) if the teacher gave assignments which 70 percent of the students did not understand, there was to be no homework for one week. At the end of one week, only two students had violated the contract and the teacher had been warned twice that the work needed more explanation before homework was given. At the end of six weeks, the obscenity had vanished, the teacher was instructing more and at a more appropriate level and pace. The contract was almost forgotten.

Resolving problems by involving students gives them choices in the way they behave. They control to some degree the solution, and in turn they are controlled by the teacher and their peers. Students decide to change and agree to change behavior. Contracts, either oral or written, are often a crucial part of the scientific approach to problem solving and can be useful even when the six-step problem-solving process is not used.

UTILIZING BEHAVIOR CONTRACTING

In many instances, especially with individual students whose behavior has to be changed in small but important steps, teachers sometimes use a written contract. A statement written by the teacher and student and agreed upon by both with written signatures can be a powerful incentive to "live up to" an agreement.

> Effective classroom managers use contracting to resolve behavior problems.

A written contract spells out exactly what is expected of the student and the teacher. It should begin with easily and quickly met agreements. A series of short contracts will provide more immediate evidence of success than an all or nothing, global agreement. Contracts should be worded in simple terms. Legal terms can confuse and intimidate students and should be avoided. (See Form 5.2.) Any contract states what both teacher and student agree to do. It also specifies the rewards if the terms of the contract are met and the consequences of failure to live up to the agreement.

Form 5.2 BEHAVIOR CONTRACT

CONTRACT

CONTRACT BETWEEN _____(student)_____ AND _____(teacher)_____ .

DATE _____

_____(student)_____ AGREES TO _____(behavior)_____ AND _____(teacher)_____

AGREES TO _____(behavior)_____

CONSEQUENCES _____ .

REWARDS _____ .

DATE FOR CHECKING PROGRESS _____ .

DATE FOR COMPLETION _____ .

SIGNATURES _____ AND _____ .

There are three major steps to negotiating contracts. First, the teacher must see to it that the problem is clearly understood by the student or group of students. Second, the student and teacher must then find alternative ways of behaving. (The suggestions given for brainstorming earlier in this chapter may be followed here.) All possible alternatives or choices, including suspension and expulsion, should be included as choices. The student and teacher must mutually agree to try one of the alternatives and must also agree on the consequences resulting from failure to meet the terms of the agreement. Third, the agreement must be written, and a copy should be given to the student. Details of the agreement should be spelled out and all expectations described in explicit terms. The student should be able verbally to state the goal of the contract and the consequence for not fulfilling the contract. Contracts should be evaluated periodically. Progress toward the goal should be assessed, and if necessary, the contract should be renegotiated. Contracts that work can be renewed, extended, and expanded; and, of course, those that fail should be renegotiated or discarded. The teacher's attitude toward the student, the contract, and the effort made to meet the terms should be one of patience and cooperation.

Contracts are most useful when used with individuals. Group contracting can be effective when the rewards are attractive; however, the failure of one student to live up to a group contract can cause problems with those students who do comply.

Contracts can be used as part of the scientific process described earlier, or they can be developed and used with individuals and groups in a somewhat incidental manner. Contracts are also used in structured approaches to changing behavior, such as programs of behavior modification.

LOOKING AT BEHAVIOR MODIFICATION

It is beyond the scope of this book to provide the necessary information and implementation strategies that would prepare teachers to use a program of behavior modification. All teachers, however, should know the theory on which this approach to improving students' conduct is based.

The foundation of behavior modification is the work of behavioral psychologists. The two best known are Ivan Pavlov and B. F. Skinner. Pavlov, as a result of his famous experiment with dogs, concluded that animal behavior was a response to stimuli in the environment. Skinner's experiments with pigeons and mice led him to apply Pavlov's stimulus-response theory of animal behavior to human behavior. Behavior modification programs for children and adults are based on the premise that human behavior is and can be shaped by environmental factors, that there is no inner rational person, and that persons who behave rationally do so because their environment has rewarded rational behavior and punished or ignored irrational behavior.

Advocates of behavior modification believe that a student's behavior can be changed by changing the environment, and they give little emphasis to understanding any underlying causes of the behavior. Behavior modification assumes that behavior is learned because it has been reinforced by someone or something in the environment. This assumption is the basis for the best-known principle of behavior modification programs—reinforce desirable behavior; punish or ignore undesirable behavior—and epitomizes the interventionists' approach to dealing with students' behavior.

Probably more research and more teacher training has been devoted to various forms of behavior modification than to any other approach to managing classrooms and teaching discipline. It is used extensively in many programs for exceptional children, and adaptations of some techniques are used by some teachers who may even find the stimulus-response theory unacceptable. Some examples of behavior modification used by teachers who do not use a total program of behavior modification are contingency contracting, modeling, reinforcing appropriate behavior with praise and tokens or other tangible rewards; many teachers practice the axiom, "Whenever possible ignore inappropriate behavior and reward appropriate behavior."

Adaptations of behavior modification strategies are used by teachers throughout the country. One such adaptation and discipline model is Assertive Discipline by Lee and Marlene Canter, mentioned in Chapter 1. Assertive discipline has been described as "not much more than applied behavior modification and take-charge teacher firmness with rules and consequences" (McDaniel, 1989). Although assertive discipline is widely used and espoused by many school administrators, many other educators voice the same objections to its use as the objections they voice to behavior modification. Some of these objections are as follows:

1. It does not attempt to understand and remove or change the origins of inappropriate behavior.
2. Behaviorists oversimplify student misconduct by attributing it almost solely to a desire for attention, and many psychologists believe students also misbehave to display inadequacy and seek power and revenge.
3. It is difficult to find appropriate reinforcers for older students and adults.
4. Ignoring inappropriate behavior may actually reinforce the behavior.
5. Students are taught to work for rewards and not for the internal satisfaction of doing a job well.
6. It emphasizes short-range instead of long-range results.

Behavior modification can be powerful and should be used with caution. Most colleges and universities offer at least one course in preparing teachers to utilize systematic behavior modification. No teacher should attempt to use such a program without professional training.

UTILIZING SOCIALIZATION

Classrooms are social groups. What teachers and students do can never be explained solely in terms of academic learning. The socialization of students is one of the primary purposes of the school; many educators and psychologists believe it is the school's most important function. In many preschools and in the early grades a formal socialization curriculum is used to teach students to participate as group members in an appropriate, acceptable manner. Games, role playing, and clarifying strategies are often used to help children learn appropriate social behavior. Whether we like it or not many students, especially at the secondary level, enjoy school only because they get to see and interact with their friends. Most students care more about these social interactions than about their academic performance (Coleman, 1961). Many students who like school develop friendships with their classmates, and students who fail to find friends often dislike school and become withdrawn or aggressive. Some students find social interaction by joining gangs. Unfortunately, gangs tend to be composed of students who fail to become socialized as members of a total classroom or school group and the gangs that they join function in antisocial ways.

Most teachers recognize the importance of socialization. Effective teachers make a concerted effort to help students function appropriately in classroom interaction. They make sure shy, reticent students are included in activities. They attempt to help students with academic, emotional, or other problems find friends; and they try to get student peers to accept students with problems.

Effective classroom managers use socialization as a way to resolve problem behavior.

Brophy and Rohrkemper (1980) found that teachers in the lower grades are more likely to use socialization as a way of resolving students' hostile and aggressive behavior than are teachers of upper grades. Some teachers, especially in secondary schools, tend to place more emphasis on methods of control that force conformity than on socialization. Forcing conformity may temporarily stop the immediate behavior but does not resolve the problem. The researchers also found that teachers who emphasized socialization as a goal of the school used rewards, peer pressure, and supportive behavior to change behavior and looked for reasons why students are antisocial.

We have already discussed the importance of modeling behavior in Chapter 2. Modeling is a powerful tool for socializing student behavior. Students tend to model behavior they see in others, and we must remember that both antisocial and social behavior was probably learned from models at home or at school. We know that teachers must model the behavior expected of students and refrain from displaying the antisocial behaviors they are trying to extinguish. Some antisocial behaviors that some teachers model are sarcasm, criticism, ridicule, vindictiveness, scapegoating, and anger. Many students learn acceptable behavior by conscious or unconscious emulation of teachers. Therefore it is important for teachers to consciously relate to students who display antisocial behavior in the way they want students to relate to them and their student peers. Direct modeling of desirable behavior was used by a teacher of an antisocial sixth grader who was easily agitated and almost always shouted at his teacher and his classmates. When he shouted or yelled, the teacher would quietly ask, "Alex, do I shout at you?" "No." "Then please try not to shout at me." After six months Alex was speaking in a normal voice.

Socialization of students' behavior is often a long process; however, for students who do not have deep-seated emotional problems and do not require counseling by school staff or other professionals there are many techniques besides modeling that effective teachers use to assist them with resolving problems. Some of the techniques suggested by experienced teachers are giving students a chance to express their opinion without passing judgment on that opinion; role-playing; having students work in pairs, tutoring one another; having students work in a group and produce a product; having students participate in cooperative learning activities; giving students some responsibilities; helping students clarify goals; and giving attention to students' seating arrangements.

Of course, the methods used will depend on the nature of a student's problem. For example, Amy was a gifted fifth grader described by her former teacher and classmates as a smart alec who called out answers when other students were called on, poked fun at students who were slower learners, gave unsolicited advice, and interfered with instruction by criticizing the teacher and other students. The teacher began to look for ways to get Amy to use her energy and knowledge in productive ways. She decided to let Amy help her with materials but only if she followed the clearly stated directions given her. Amy responded well and seemed to enjoy the job. After conferencing, Amy and the teacher decided that Amy could "tutor" some of the other children in math, but only as long as she followed directions given her by the teacher and if her peers agreed. Amy's critical attitude became more positive, her peers began to accept her, and Amy found some friends.

Jeff was a seventh grade student whose behavior in social studies was described as inattentive—he would create funny noises, trip others, refuse to do work, and ignore teacher requests. Six weeks after school began Jeff's teacher showed an old but excellent film on colonial America. Jeff was seated beside the old movie projector and appeared interested in how the machine worked. He asked questions about the machine, film, videotapes, and other equipment. The teacher told Jeff he would be glad to teach him how to use the audio equipment located in the media center if he would be interested. Jeff indicated that he was interested, and the teacher arranged some time to work with Jeff. Three 30-minute sessions were enough for him to become expert in operating all the machines, and thereafter when a film or video was shown, Jeff was the operator. His antisocial behavior stopped, and his academic work improved.

These two examples of solutions to problems may appear too easy and obviously simple, but teachers should be reassured to know that some problems can be resolved quickly, even though many take time, energy, and intense attention. Some students will need professional counseling in order to function in acceptable ways; and teachers also need to realize that, in spite of all their efforts, some students fail to develop the skills and attitudes to function acceptably and successfully in our society.

UTILIZING PUNISHMENT

In Chapter 1, punishment was defined as an unpleasant, painful consequence aimed at altering inappropriate behavior and based on the notion of inflicting harm or inducing pain. The research evidence indicates that "punishment can control misbehavior, but by itself it will not teach desirable behavior or even reduce the desire to misbehave" (Good and Brophy, 1987). In a summary of the research literature on the effectiveness of punishment Weber, et al. (1983) state that "punishment is a managerial strategy about which there is widespread disagreement." Some see the appropriate use of punishment as an effective way to stop misbehavior; others say the careful use of appropriate punishment in certain situations can have short-term positive effects, but negative side effects must be considered; still others say punishment should never be used under any circumstances. Those who believe in the interventionist theory of child development, and those who believe in the stimulus-response principle (behaviorists), see punishment as an effective strategy for dealing with behavior problems, whereas persons with other philosophical views of human behavior do not. The research literature suggests that mild forms of desists, reprimands, and so on, which are viewed by some as punishment, are effective in dealing with behavior problems whereas harsh forms of punishment, such as physical punishment, are not effective (Weber, et al. 1983). The use of harsh punishment by teachers to manage classrooms and teach discipline is highly controversial; and in spite of the research evidence, some teachers continue to use punishment of all types, ranging from mild to harsh.

Effective classroom managers avoid harsh punishment.

Harsh punishment can be anything that harms or inflicts emotional or physical pain. It can be a simple statement that embarrasses or ridicules in a hurtful way. A statement like, "How would you like to go stay with your little sister in her kindergarten class?" can inflict a powerful wound to an older student. Many adults still remember with great pain a teacher who embarrassed them. Teachers should remember that a blow to the ego or "below the belt" can be harsh. Many psychologists agree that emotional pain can be more harsh and harmful than physical pain.

There is little doubt that in many if not most classrooms some form of consequences for inappropriate behavior is meted out. No matter if the procedure is called "suffering the consequences," "being disciplined," or "receiving punishment," the following general guidelines will serve to make the action more effective in stopping misbehavior and developing self-control.

1. Any discipline measure should be administered as soon as possible after the undesirable behavior. The longer the delay between the behavior and disciplinary action, the less effective discipline becomes.

2. Each situation that requires a disciplinary measure should be

considered in terms of the offending behavior and the student's age and individuality.

3. The discipline measure should be understood by and meaningful to the student.
4. A discipline measure should be consistently applied for inappropriate behavior and in terms of the situation; it should not depend on the mood of the teacher.
5. The discipline measure should be administered as privately as possible.
6. If discipline measures must be administered, then information should be given so that the student will know how to behave next time.
7. Do not stay angry with students who are punished. Help a student return to normal activities as soon as possible, and reconcile any anger or resentment between you and the student.
8. Do not punish entire groups because of the behavior of a few.
9. Discipline measures should be taken only after repeated misbehavior that in the view of the teacher must be stopped. Punishment is inappropriate when dealing with isolated incidents if you think the behavior will not be repeated.
10. Discipline measures should be avoided when students are trying to behave appropriately.
11. Never use extra assignments to discipline. It teaches students that learning is punishment instead of enjoyment.

Discipline measures vary in form and degree of severity. Some students perceive even a mild desist as punishment. Reprimands, after school conferences between teacher and student, detention, payment for destroyed property, isolation, suspension, and expulsion from school can be used to punish. The harshest forms of punishment are suspensions, expulsions, and physical punishment.

Corporal Punishment

Physical punishment, often called *corporal punishment*, is controversial and is not recommended by most psychologists and educators. In addition to its lack of effectiveness in changing behavior, it has many significant side effects including (1) it may increase disruptive behavior; (2) it may hinder learning; (3) it may develop hostility; (4) it is often administered because the teacher is frustrated; (5) it teaches that the strong intimidate the weak; (6) it teaches that might makes right; and (7) many psychologists and educators say it is not suitable for any child of any size, age, or socioeconomic status.

Although corporal punishment is illegal in many states, some school systems permit its use but generally have explicit guidelines as to how and by whom it can be administered. In some districts it can be administered only by a school administrator, in the presence of witnesses, after a "cooling off" period has elapsed; and the instrument used must be the hand. In spite of its illegality and strictly supervised use, some teachers and administrators continue to hit, pinch, twist arms, and shove students.

The National School Public Relations Council (1976), in a bulletin entitled *Discipline Crisis in Schools*, reported that one old German schoolmaster kept an exact record for 51 years of his disciplinary measures and found that he had

> . . . struck 911,527 blows with a cane, 124,010 with a rod, 20,989 with a ruler, 136,715 with his hand, 12,235 blows to the mouth, 7,905 boxes to the ear, and 1,115,800 raps on the head—in addition to making 777 boys stand on peas, 613 kneel on a triangular block of wood, and 5,000 wear a dunce's cap.

In today's world and democratic classrooms, it would be more appropriate for teachers to keep a record of their positive approaches to inappropriate student behavior.

Form 5.3 DO'S AND DON'TS OF RESOLVING PROBLEMS

1. DO discuss problems.	1. DON'T over-discuss.
2. DO act to solve problems.	2. DON'T threaten to act to solve problems.
3. DO let students "save face" when they are in a tight place.	3. DON'T embarrass and ridicule students.
4. DO negotiate contracts with students.	4. DON'T make deals or offer bribes.
5. DO punish students who must be punished, but not harshly.	5. DON'T punish a total class.
6. DO reprimand in private.	6. DON'T publicly embarrass students.
7. DO discuss, or walk away from students.	7. DON'T argue.
8. DO be supportive of students' efforts to resolve problems.	8. DON'T remain aloof from students' problems.
9. DO assume some responsibility for helping students with problem behavior.	9. DON'T ignore students' problems.
10. DO try to manage your own classroom and students' problems.	10. DON'T rely on administrators to resolve problems in your classroom.

Suspensions and Expulsions

Suspension and expulsion are two disciplinary measures used when a student's behavior is so disruptive or out of control that the student needs to be removed from the classroom. *Suspension* means temporary removal from the classroom or school for a day or more; *expulsion* is permanent removal from the school.

Suspension and expulsion are drastic measures. Teachers should make every effort to work constructively with a student before recommending or going along with either procedure. Suspending or expelling students usually means students (1) miss schoolwork, which increases their chance of failure; (2) do not receive help from school personnel with their emotional, physical, or academic problems; (3) are rewarded for inappropriate behavior because many of them want to leave school; (4) tend to hang around the school and cause trouble; and (5) do not appear to change their behavior as a result of suspension or expulsion.

Many forward-looking school systems provide special schools and in-school suspension rooms for seriously disruptive students who must be removed from the regular classroom. Teachers should be familiar with the school policies regarding suspension and expulsion, alternative facilities, and other avenues available to help them and their students. Many school systems have a systemwide code of student conduct and a list of recommended and even mandatory procedures for dealing with inappropriate and unacceptable conduct. Teachers should always follow school policy in regard to administering disciplinary measures; if they are philosophically opposed to such policies, then they should find a position in a school district where policies are compatible with their own views.

SUMMARY

In this chapter general strategies supported by research findings as effective in resolving behavior problems have been discussed. The suggested principles of resolving problems can be effective when applied in a supportive classroom environment and when the rapport between teacher and students is trusting.

Specifically, we have said:

1. Effective managers use desisting behaviors to resolve many common behavior problems. Desists are also used to prevent misbehavior.
2. Effective managers change the environment to resolve problems. The environment can prevent or contribute to problems. Changing it is often a simple way to resolve problems.
3. One of the best ways to resolve problems with one student or with an entire classroom group is the "scientific approach" to problem solving. This approach gives students a voice in the solution to problems. Research evidence suggests that effective managers use problem-solving approaches to resolving problems.
4. Effective managers use behavior contracting to resolve problems. Contracts are easily written to specify responsibilities of both teacher and students.
5. Although behavior modification is a controversial approach to resolving problems, effective managers use some principles derived from this approach, such as using rewards and withdrawal of privileges.
6. Effective managers use socialization of students to resolve behavior problems. Methods of socialization range from simple to complex and long-term approaches.
7. Effective managers avoid harsh punishment. If punishment is used, it is administered with care and takes into account the individuality of the student. Guidelines for administering punishment are given. Corporal punishment should not be used. The use of suspension and expulsion should also be avoided and used only if a student's behavior is endangering himself, herself, or others.
8. The methods teachers use to resolve problems should be consistent with school policy.

In the next chapter more will be said about school policy and resources to assist teachers and students in resolving problems; however, the primary focus of Chapter 6 is teaching students self-discipline.

QUESTIONS AND ACTIVITIES

5.1   Observe a teacher for an entire day, or two or more class periods, and:
      (a) list the desists that were used and were effective,
      (b) list students who responded positively to the desists, and
      (c) list students who failed to respond to the teacher's desists.
      Observe these two groups of students and look for insights into any
      differences in the students background, achievement, or other
      characteristics.

5.2   If possible observe in an elementary and secondary classroom. Compare
      desists used by the teachers. List desists that were most effective with
      each level of students.

5.3   After observing for a day, or two or more class periods, list ways the
      teacher made changes in the classroom environment. Would you have
      made the same changes? Would you have made other changes? Why?

5.4   Choose a behavior problem you have seen or encountered in your own
      teaching. Write a plan to utilize the "scientific process" of problem
      solving as an approach to resolve the problem.

5.5   Write a contract designed to change a problem behavior.

5.6   Make a list of five problem behaviors. Suggest an appropriate
      socialization strategy to resolve each behavior.

5.7   Describe a student and his or her problem behavior that you believe
      must be stopped by using punishment.

5.8   Make a list of behaviors for teachers to avoid when they administer
      discipline measures.

5.9   How do you feel about punishment? Under what circumstances, if any,
      would you punish a student?

5.10 "Epidemics" of inappropriate behavior sometimes break out in
      classrooms, such as throwing paper airplanes, smoking on the
      playground, stamping feet, calling out, giggling for reasons unknown to
      the teacher. What strategy would you use for dealing with such an
      epidemic?

5.11 A fourth grader copies from his classmate's paper and is repeatedly
      reminded not to do so. The teacher has decided the student is a "cheat"
      and needs to be punished. Reminding the student not to copy has not
      stopped the behavior. What should the teacher do now?

5.12 Draw up a contract to use with one student. Choose one of these
      problem behaviors to change: talking out without permission, being
      tardy, or failing to bring materials, books, or other supplies to class. Or,
      choose one of your own.

5.13 A tenth grade English teacher stood beside the open door to her classroom. Students in the second period class entered as usual. An assistant principal stopped to talk and detained the teacher about four minutes after the bell rang. When the teacher entered the room, she found most of the students laughing loudly. Five students were out of their seats and racing through the room. Three or four were pounding desks with their books.

The teacher has to deal with this situation. Some options might be:

1. She enters the room, pounds her desk, and in a loud, irritated voice says, "Get your paper and pencil. We are going to have a test. You know better than to behave this way."

2. She enters the room, walks to her desk, and says in a calm voice, "Take your seats. Be quiet. Before we begin today's lesson, let's briefly review our rules of conduct and the consequences for breaking the rules."

3. She decides to draw up a behavioral contract, which will specify student behavior.

4. She decides to use the "scientific process" of problem solving and begins a discussion to define the problem.

5. She enters the room and ignores the entire incident.

(a) What are the advantages (if any) and disadvantages (if any) to each of the above options?

(b) Write another option for the teacher.

(c) What does each option reveal about the teacher's concept of discipline and management?

REFERENCES

Axelrod, S. (1977). *Behavior Modification for the Classroom Teacher*. New York: McGraw-Hill.

Brophy, J. (1985). "Classroom Management as Instruction: Socializing Self-Guidance in Students." *Theory into Practice, 24*, pp. 233–240.

Brophy, J. (1986). *Socializing Student Motivation to Learn*. (Research Series No. 169.) East Lansing, Mich.: College of Education, Michigan State University, Institute for Research on Teaching.

Brophy, J., and Rohrkemper, M. (1980). *Teachers' Specific Strategies for Dealing with Hostile, Aggressive Students*. (Research Series No. 86.) East Lansing, Mich.: Michigan State University, Institute for Research on Teaching, pp. 38–40, 40–42.

Brophy, J., and Rohrkemper, M. (1981). "The Influence of Problem Ownership on Teachers' Perceptions of and Strategies for Coping with Problem Students." *Journal of Educational Psychology, 73*, pp. 295–311.

Brophy, J., and Rohrkemper, M. (1988). "The Classroom Strategy Study: Summary Report of General Findings." (Research Series No. 187.) East Lansing, Mich.: Michigan State University, Institute for Research on Teaching.

Canter, L. (1988). "Let the Educator Beware: A Response to Curwin and Mendler." *Educational Leadership, 46* (2), pp. 71–73.

Canter, L., and Canter, M. (1976). *Assertive Discipline: A Take-Charge Approach for Today's Educator.* Los Angeles, Calif.: Lee Canter and Associates.

Charles, C. (1985). *Building Classroom Discipline: From Models to Practice.* New York: Longman.

Coleman, J. (1961). *The Adolescent Society: The Social Life of the Teenager and Its Impact on Education.* New York: Free Press.

Curwin, R., and Mendler, A. (1988). "Packaged Discipline Programs: Let the Buyer Beware." *Educational Leadership, 46* (2), pp. 68–71.

Dreikurs, R., and Cassel, P. (1972). *Discipline Without Tears.* New York: Hawthorn Books.

Dreikurs, R., Grunwald, B., and Pepper, F. (1982). *Maintaining Sanity in the Classroom: Management Techniques.* New York: Harper and Row.

Gartrell, D. (1987). "Assertive Discipline: Unhealthy for Children and Other Living Things." *Young Children, 42* (2), pp. 10–11.

Ginott, H. (1972). *Teacher and Child.* New York: Macmillan.

Glasser, W. (1965). *Reality Therapy.* New York: Harper and Row.

Glasser, W. (1969). *Schools without Failure.* New York: Harper and Row.

Good, T., and Brophy, J. (1987). *Looking in Classrooms* (4th ed.). New York: Harper and Row, p. 269.

Gordon, T. (1974). *TET Teacher Effectiveness Training.* New York: David McKay, pp. 227–249, 136–155.

Hamilton, S. (1983). "Synthesis of Research on the Social Side of Schooling." *Educational Leadership, 40* (5), pp. 65–72.

Homme, L. (1970). *How to Use Contingency Contracting in the Classroom.* Champaign, Ill.: Research Press.

Johnson, D., and Johnson, R. (1990). "Social Skills for a Successful Group Work." *Educational Leadership, 47* (4), pp. 29–33.

Kounin, J. (1970). *Discipline and Group Management in Classrooms.* New York: Holt, Rinehart and Winston.

Madsen, C. H., and Madsen, C. K. (1970). *Teaching Discipline: Behavioral Principles Toward a Positive Approach.* Boston: Allyn and Bacon.

McDaniel, T. (1989). "The Discipline Debate: A Road Through the Thicket." *Educational Leadership, 46* (6), p. 82.

Medlick, J. (1979). *Effective Classroom Strategies for Three Problem Behaviors: Hostile-Aggressive, Passive-Aggressive and Withdrawn Failure-Image.* (Occasional Paper No. 30.) East Lansing, Mich.: Michigan State University, Institute for Research on Teaching.

National School Public Relations Council (1976). *Discipline Crisis in Schools.* Arlington, Va.: National School Public Relations Council.

Prawat, R., and Nickerson, J. (1985). "Relationship Between Teacher Thought and Action and Student Affective Outcomes." *Elementary School Journal, 85,* pp. 529–540.

Raths, L., Harmin, M., and Simon, S. (1966). *Values and Teaching*. Columbus, Ohio: Charles E. Merrill.

Render, G., Padilla, J., and Krank, M. (1989). "What Research Really Shows about Assertive Discipline." *Educational Leadership, 46* (6), pp. 72–75.

Schwartz, S. (1990). *Coping with Crisis Situations in the Classroom*. Englewood Cliffs, N.J.: Prentice-Hall.

Sheffield, A., and Frankel, B. (eds.) (1989). *When I Was Young, I Loved School*. New York: Children's Express Foundation.

Skinner, B. F. (1953). *Science and Human Behavior*. New York: Macmillan.

Slavin, R. (1990a). "Research on Cooperative Learning: Consensus and Controversy." *Educational Leadership, 47* (4), pp. 52–54.

Slavin, R. (1990b). *Cooperative Learning: Theory, Research and Practice*. Englewood Cliffs, N.J.: Prentice-Hall.

Toner, I., Moore, L., and Emmons, B. (1980). "The Effect of Being Labeled on Subsequent Self-Control in Children." *Child Development, 51*, pp. 618–621.

Walker, J., and Shea, T. (1976). *Behavior Modification: A Practical Approach for Educators*. St. Louis, Mo.: C. V. Mosby.

Weber, W., Crawford, J., Roff, L. and Robinson, C. (1983). *Classroom Management: Reviews of the Teacher Education and Research Literature*. Princeton, N.J.: Educational Testing Service, pp. 20–42.

Chapter
6

Teaching Discipline

INTRODUCTION AND OBJECTIVES

Just as teachers of all age levels have academic goals based on curriculum guidelines and students' achievement levels, they should also have behavioral goals based on group and individual student behavioral levels. For example, teachers should recognize and understand levels and stages of behavior the same as they recognize and understand reading levels; and just as they teach reading skills and expect progress in reading achievement, they should also teach discipline and expect progress in the acquisition of appropriate behavior and self-discipline.

The teacher's immediate goal for student behavior may simply be an orderly, well managed classroom; however, the ultimate goal should be an orderly classroom where students willingly behave in appropriate ways. Seeing to it that students make progress in the acquisition of self-discipline is fundamental to successful, effective management. After self-discipline is taught, anything can be taught; and until self-discipline is learned, anything learned is worthless. Of course, maintaining and nurturing a classroom climate in which self-discipline can flourish requires a teacher who has the attributes discussed in Chapter 2, utilizes principles of effective management, and is self-disciplined.

> Effective classroom managers model and teach self-discipline.

After completing this chapter preservice and beginning teachers will be able to:

- describe teacher behaviors that model self-discipline;
- describe and utilize management behaviors that enable students to practice appropriate behavior;
- describe and utilize techniques and classroom interactions that make it possible to avoid using punishment;
- describe and utilize alternatives to punishment;
- describe and utilize ways to avoid criticism;
- describe and utilize ways to avoid conflicts with students;
- describe and utilize appropriate feedback;
- describe and utilize appropriate praise;
- describe and utilize procedures that hold students accountable;
- list and describe characteristics of an effective grading system;
- list procedures for helping students understand a grading system, and
- list behaviors, procedures, and methods discussed in previous chapters which nurture and encourage self-discipline.

In Chapter 1 discipline was defined as teacher behavior intended to create and maintain conditions essential to (1) the orderly work of teaching and learning and (2) the development of student self-control. The foci of Chapters 2, 3, 4, and 5 have been teacher behaviors that prevent and resolve inappropriate student behavior and encourage appropriate behavior. Ideally, if teachers have the characteristics described in Chapter 2 and utilize principles of effective management and discipline listed in the following chapters, students will learn self-discipline. The purpose of Chapter 6 is to suggest ways teachers can provide students with the classroom climate, knowledge, and skills necessary to manager their own behavior and practice self-discipline.

What is self-discipline? It is controlling one's own behavior without constant and continuous reminders from teachers, parents, supervisors, police officers or "who ever is in charge." When students learn self-discipline they understand the importance and advantages of self-control. They realize that they accomplish tasks more quickly and enjoy learning and living more when they are in control. At the same time, they are aware of the consequences of their behavior in relation to the group. They are cognizant of the importance of the group, whether it be their family, their classroom, their school, or the larger society. Self-discipline not only affects the individual, it also affects the group. For example, one tenant in a complex of 90 apartments bought a cat, even though cats were forbidden. The manager reminded her of the rule and asked her to get rid of the cat. The tenant was indignant, "What harm could one cat do?" The manager replied, "You are absolutely right. One cat is not a problem, but imagine the problem if each tenant owned a cat." The tenant agreed that 90 cats would present a serious problem.

The productive functioning of any individual and any group depends on self-discipline. Self-discipline enables students to function socially and academically in a productive and acceptable manner; it is essential to living in the world as well as in classrooms. One way students learn appropriate behavior, including—and perhaps especially—self-control is from influential persons who serve as models.

MODELING SELF-DISCIPLINE

> Effective Classroom managers model self-discipline.

Some of the effects of modeling have been discussed in Chapter 2, but the importance and power of modeling cannot be overemphasized. It has already been stated that the ability to model self-discipline is essential to teaching self-discipline; any management and discipline plan that works has to be implemented by a teacher who demonstrates the behaviors she or he expects of students.

Curwin and Mendler (1988) summarize an effective discipline plan in the following way:

> . . . a truly effective discipline plan must include, but go beyond, rules, rewards, consequences, and punishments. It must send a message of respect, dignity, belief, and hope to those most directly affected.

If this is true, modeling may be the only way to include dimensions of discipline that go beyond enforcing rules and regulations and practice. Teachers should remember that students learn more from models than from critics. Teachers who model self-discipline treat students in the manner they themselves expect to be treated.

HELPING STUDENTS PRACTICE SELF-DISCIPLINE

Teachers who model and practice self-discipline understand that perfection is worked toward but seldom achieved. Even the most secure and mature teachers with powerful ego strength have valleys and peaks of self-control and must continually work toward refining and perfecting their own behavior. The nature of human beings and their environment make it necessary to continuously practice restraining our inappropriate actions and reinforcing our appropriate behavior. Effective managers model appropriate behaviors and create classroom conditions that allow, encourage, and require students to practice self-control. Perfection is always a goal to be achieved.

Effective classroom managers make it possible for students to practice appropriate behavior.

Practicing appropriate behavior can be flagrantly obvious or ingeniously subtle. Teachers often have young students practice such things as talking quietly, walking in halls, using a knife and fork; and the students are told they are practicing correct behavior and why. On the other hand, and especially with older students, practicing behavior and conditions that encourage or require appropriate behavior can and should be more subtle. For example, a junior high school teacher who taught 35 students in a classroom designed for 20 found that students were tempted to look at other students' test papers. Testing became an unmanageable activity. She found herself threatening, moralizing, and even trying to "catch" students who copied; when none of these approaches worked, she began to look for ways to change the testing situation. The solution she found was easy and simple. She devised two forms of the same test by reversing the order of the items; that is, on a test of 50 items, item 50 on the first version became item 1 on the second form of the test. To make it easier to administer the test, she had the school secretary copy form 1 on blue paper and form 2 on pink paper. Every other student was given a blue test, and the others were given a pink test. Students kept their eyes on their own papers, and the problem was eliminated. Toward the end of the year when she went back to one form for all students, they continued to keep their eyes on their own papers. The practice of appropriate behavior continued. Who knows, perhaps many of them realized they needed no help.

Effective managers provide opportunities for practicing self-discipline that are both subtle and powerful. Teachers who have this ability are like David in the Old Testament, who slew the giant with a small stone. They use the right word and the right action at the right time. They exude class, charm, respect, and authority simultaneously. They provide students with opportunities to "save face" and give them insights into behavior and the consequences of that behavior. Their aim is not "to catch" students misbehaving and punish them, but to give students opportunities to behave appropriately. A singular characteristic of these teachers is they recognize that the acquisition of self-discipline by students must be measured by the progress made and not by perfection; therefore, in addition to serving as models, they willingly assist students with the practice of appropriate behavior as an alternative to punishment.

FINDING ALTERNATIVES TO PUNISHMENT

> Effective classroom managers seek alternatives to punishment.

Researchers and philosophers have identified characteristics and behaviors of teachers who encourage and teach discipline, but none has been a more skillful advocate or stated their thoughts with more power, succinctness, and flair than Haim Ginott (1972). He believed punishment was not only useless but indeed harmful to both teachers and students. He says:

Punishment does not deter misconduct. It merely makes the offender more cautious in committing his crime, more adroit in concealing his traces, more skillful in escaping detection.

Punishment is pointless. It fails to achieve its goal.

There is always danger in punishment. It breeds brutality—sadistic or masochistic.

Discipline is not a matter of fitting punishment to crime and balancing books. It is the teacher's generosity, not his accuracy, that counts.

One grows into virtue; one cannot be forced by punishment.

The essence of discipline is finding alternatives to punishment. To punish a child is to enrage him and make him uneducable.[1]

Psychologists such as Ginott are not alone in their rejection of punishment as a useful tool. In Chapter 5 we learned that research evidence also indicates that punishment may stop or control misbehavior but does not teach students how to behave (Good and Brophy, 1987). If the essence of discipline is finding alternatives to punishment, then the essence of finding alternatives to punishment is careful, purposeful, caring dialogue between teachers and students.

Avoiding Criticism

Effective classroom managers avoid criticism.

Criticism destroys self-concept and self-confidence and does not encourage self-discipline. It comes in many forms—a sarcastic remark, "You're so intelligent," when a student gives an incorrect response; a question, "Why do you always misbehave?"; a joke at the student's expense, "Hello, Grumpy!" A statement of fact made in a harsh tone such as, "That's not right," or "Don't ask me again," is not only destructive to students' ego strength, it also undermines the possibility of productive, rewarding relationships with students. Criticism not only

---

[1]Reprinted from H. Ginott, *Teacher and Child*, pp. 147–152.

hurts students and student-teacher relationships, it also leads to the erosion of teacher power and authority.

Most teachers know that criticism is not helpful, but they use it to "defend" themselves. They use it to exert influence and exercise authority. They use it to let students know they can "have the last word" and that they are in charge or know more than the student. They also use it for revenge and to put students down, but they also use it without thinking. They get caught in the criticism trap. Students misbehave, the teachers criticizes, and students respond to the criticism with more misconduct. For example, a student teacher whose comments to students were frequently critical found that criticism can be a two-edged sword. Her third grade students persisted in shouting out answers without raising hands. After students were asked a question and had yelled out for permission to answer, the teacher called on Carole. Joseph, a clever student who knew the teacher's supervisor was observing, quickly answered before Carole could respond. The teacher said, "Is your name Carole?" Joseph, enthusiastically replied, "Yes!" Now, where does the teacher go from here? Imagine the administrator's reaction if Joseph is sent to the office for telling the teacher his name is Carole! Criticism makes students feel inadequate, powerless, and angry; it makes the teacher a petty, destructive ,vulnerable, "little" person.

Some teachers object to seemingly simplistic alternatives to criticism because they feel teachers appear weak and powerless, but many of these simplistic-appearing approaches work. They often resolve the specific situation and prevent the recurrence of the behavior. Many teachers find that the following alternatives work in specific situations.

1. When any incident has some element of humor, such as a harmless prank, laugh with the students. Don't search for the offender or punish or criticize the entire class. Denouncing behavior can encourage it.
2. When students use four-letter words, a stern look is often more effective than a lecture. No talk can be more powerful than a lot of talk.
3. When an inappropriate behavior occurs rarely or once in a blue moon, it may be possible to ignore it.
4. When a behavior such as tipping over a chair or letting a door slam appears to be accidental, clear eye contact can serve as a reminder to students to watch what they are doing. If you

make a big deal of it, slamming doors may become a common occurrence.

5. When the whole class is excited and acting out their excitement about a situation or even an occurrence such as unusual weather or a story in the news, instead of criticizing have students write a composition about their feelings or some aspect of the happening.

6. When infractions of rules or failure to follow procedures occurs, quietly remind students of the rules and procedures.

7. Remove objects that may be causing disputes, such as globes, rulers, or other objects. Students can learn to take turns using materials.

8. When a student is frustrated or angry, let the student know you recognize her or his feelings. Say, "I see you are very angry. Let us wait to talk about this."

9. Tell students how you feel about an incident, not the student. "I am surprised at this mess," can be more effective than calling students slobs.

10. When students disagree with each other they often resort to violence. When this happens have them write "their side of the story" instead of telling it to the teacher. Writing can often calm and clarify turbulent thoughts.

11. When a student breaks a rule, don't accuse him or her of deliberate misbehavior. Tell the student you will help him or her remember the rule.

An effective alternative to criticism is correction. Correction that is given automatically, willingly, and with respect for the student can trigger student efforts to improve or stop behaviors. Most students find it difficult to be rude when help is offered in a spirit of concern and respect. For example, a student came to class without his math book. The teacher said, "You never have your book. Where is it? Can't you find it? You can't function in this class without that book." In another classroom, a student announced to her teacher that she had no math book that day. The teacher said, "You may use my book when we do the practice exercises. Perhaps another student will share with you while I am using mine. Bring your book tomorrow. You know we use it every day."

Correcting and helping is far more productive than criticism. The second teacher is on the road to solving the problem of the missing book and is reminding the student of responsible behavior. The first teacher has only created more problems; the second teacher is teaching discipline.

Avoiding Student-Teacher Conflicts

> Effective classroom managers avoid student-teacher conflicts.

Criticism often leads to student reactions that are more disruptive than the behavior that precipitated the criticism. Criticism can cause anger and defensiveness, which often prompt behavior so disruptive and serious the teacher feels it calls for punishment. These reactions make it difficult or impossible for students to practice appropriate behavior and learn self-control. For example, (1) asking students questions such as, "Why did you do this?" (2) "Why did you do such a stupid thing?" (3) arguing with students, or (4) preaching a sermon about a minor incident when a word would do can all cause student-teacher conflict, even confrontations. Self-discipline is not easily practiced by either students or teachers when the classroom atmosphere is filled with conflict or scarred with confrontations.

A classic example of avoiding student-teacher conflicts and finding an alternative to punishment and criticism is provided by Haim Ginott (1972).

To Save a Soul

The following story has a simple but universal moral: Kindness can only be taught kindly. Andy, age eight, was the scapegoat of his class. Children ganged up on him with insults and attacks. The chief bully and mischief-maker was Jay, age nine. When his teacher learned about this behavior, she became furious. Her first impulse was to punish him severely, "to give him a dose of his own medicine."

But she stopped herself. She explained, "I did not want to display more cruelty. He did not need an additional taste of the jungle. What he needed was a demonstration of civilization." To avoid arguments and to leave a more lasting impression, the teacher wrote Jay a note instead of arranging a face-to-face talk. The letter read:

Dear Jay,

Andy's mother has told me that her son has been made very unhappy this year. Name-calling and ostracizing have left him sad and lonely. I feel concerned about the situation. Your experience as a leader in your class makes you a likely person for me to turn to for advice. I value your ability to sympathize with those who suffer. Please write me your suggestions about how we can help Andy.

Sincerely,
Your Teacher

Jay never replied in writing, but his attacks on Andy ceased.[2]

In this incident the teacher refrained from criticizing Jay; instead she displayed the kind of behavior he needed to display with Andy. She decided he needed to be exposed to a "civilized" method of dealing with others. A simple note avoided criticism and an angry confrontation with Jay. Confrontations are characterized by critical and argumentative statements. When teachers argue with students, they abandon their role of effective teachers and their authority vanishes. Effective teachers take control of problem situations and do not become a part of them. They know arguments give credibility to the students' position and do not result in meaningful dialogue. Angry confrontations undermine trust between the teacher and students, the credibility of the teacher, the self-concept of the students, and the learning climate. In addition, neither criticism nor confrontations are effective in stopping disruptive behavior and offer no opportunity to teach and learn self-discipline. Critical, angry verbal exchanges should certainly be avoided.

Praise

Research on the effects of praise is extensive; and the findings indicate, surprisingly, that it may not be as effective in reinforcing student behavior as many educators and psychologists once thought. In order to be effective, praise must have all the characteristics for effective feedback listed in Chapter 5 *and more*.

---

[2]Reprinted from H. Ginott, *Teacher and Child*, pp. 167–168.

> Effective classroom managers use praise effectively to teach discipline.

Generally speaking, research on praise by teachers indicates that if praise is effective it must be simple, direct, specific, private, and contingent on accomplishment; and it must be used sparingly. Effective managers know that the quality of praise appears to be more important than the quantity (Brophy, 1979). They also recognize that students' developmental levels and social maturity determine the effectiveness of praise as a reinforcer of student behavior. They know that praise is more likely to be reinforcing for young children up to ages seven or eight than for older students. When students outgrow the need to please adults and become more concerned with peer approval, praise from the teacher may no longer be a reinforcer and may even be counterproductive. Therefore, effective managers find nonpublic ways to show students, especially older students, that they appreciate and approve of their behavior. A private comment given quickly and genuinely, a private smile, or a note can be powerful if the teacher has attractive power and is perceived as credible.

Praise may be more effective as a reinforcer with some students than others. Some students of low ability or low socioeconomic status, minority students, and introverted students may be more likely to respond positively to teacher praise than extroverts will. Students of all ages, ability, socioeconomic status, and ethnic groups who care about and are influenced by the approval of others are more likely to respond to praise than students who form their own opinions and determine their own behavior (Brophy, 1979). For example, a student in the early stages of a graduate program was reluctant to talk in class and appeared shy and introverted. His written assignments showed effort and superior understanding, and the instructor wrote a note on one of his papers that indicated that his work demonstrated exceptional insight into the application of the content taught. The student replied with a note of his own written on his next assignment, "Thanks for your encouragement and for really making me feel special, unique, and valuable. I needed that."

Some teachers have difficulty finding words to recognize students' praiseworthy behavior. Glowing generalities such as "good work," "great," and "terrific" are not specific. Write a list of phrases you can use in specific situations or even for a specific student. Practice using these phrases. You may also want to be sure that certain students and specific behaviors are reinforced. This can be done by writing signs, such as "Praise Sammy," "Be specific," or "Praise improvement" on your plan book or other materials that only you will see, to remind you to praise in appropriate ways. Effective praise has to be practiced; many teachers need specific help to learn how to praise effectively. One teacher learned the characteristics of effective praise and decided to try more effective methods of praising students. She described her feelings and efforts to change in the following way:

> Isn't it funny how something that is supposed to come as naturally as praise is so easy to "mess up." I've always operated under the assumption that no student was praised too much. I've always thought that sometimes the praise a student gets in my class is the only good thing the student hears about himself or herself all day—maybe all week. Thus, praise was always profusely streaming out of my mouth for any behavior, any answer, any positive action. It was not until recently that I realized I was undermining my entire purpose in giving praise. If praise is supposed to make a child feel good about himself, then what I was doing was in fact destroying my credibility, and I knew something had to change.
>
> I have since learned that praise must be specific. A generalized "good" does little good, if not harm. I learned that praise must be used carefully, because if every action gets praised, then there is nothing for the student to work for. I also learned that praise can be a tool to incite hard work, good behavior, and positive action, and not just words intended to make a child feel better about himself or herself. For praise to be effective, it must be used correctly. Thus, it came time to try to change my ways.
>
> In order to change my methods of praising, I got a list of 100 ways to say "good job" without actually saying it. So, instead of saying the familiar phrase, "Good work," to each student on each paper, I found ways of using variety, of mixing it up so students didn't feel like I was following a formula. Next, for every bit of praise I gave, I amended the statement with why the action, answer, or behavior was worthy of praise. I soon found that the actual action that was praised was repeated more often because the student knew what she or he had done that was praiseworthy. Finally, I limited my praise to an individual student's behavior. In other words, the same action from every student did not get praise. The praise was dependent on the capabilities of the student. If a student usually made an "A", then praise for 100 percent correct would be more effective than praise for barely making the "A" that the student always made anyway.

A characteristic of reflective praise which I found interesting was the fact that praise should be given privately. But, being a high school teacher, I understand that secondary school students would rather please their peers than the teacher, and that public praise may curtail the desired behavior. A quiet, "Good organization on your essay," on the way out of the room may be more effective than a loud, booming, "Fine job," in the middle of class.

Although research findings indicate that praise is not the powerful reinforcer of student behavior it once was thought, if used appropriately it can be a positive force for reinforcing some students' work and attitudes at all levels. In addition, there may be some value to using praise in order to create a warm and friendly classroom climate, especially in the lower grades (Brophy, 1979). A classroom climate in which praise is used effectively can contribute to students' motivation willingly to learn self-control as well as academics.

HOLDING STUDENTS ACCOUNTABLE

Teachers who hold students accountable for their behavior and learning provide opportunities for students to learn self-discipline.

> Effective classroom managers hold students accountable for their behavior.

When teachers hold students accountable they "see to it" that students complete work on time and in acceptable form and that students behave appropriately. They also make it possible for students to act in this manner without constant supervision. Effective managers want students to be internally motivated to achieve educational goals and behave appropriately on their own. They realize that "voluntary" student involvement in learning is achieved in classrooms where interesting things are taking place, where students understand that the work they are expected to do and the behavior they are expected to demonstrate is directly related to educational goals. Effective teachers and managers avoid "busy work," which is boring and perceived as useless. In other words, effective managers help students see the importance of compliance with rules and procedures, completing work, practicing skills, doing projects, and participating in daily instruction. When students see the value of those things for which they are held accountable, they are more willing to comply with rules and teacher requests; ultimately they are more likely to learn and behave appropriately on their own. They begin to regulate their own behavior, and motivation becomes internal rather than external. Effective managers structure their instruction and interactions with students to provide opportunities for students to make choices, explore their own interests, and satisfy their curiosity; they find ways to reward students for those behaviors. They know that holding students accountable is fundamental to effective management and learning. They also know that students tend to live up to teacher expectations, academically and behaviorally, when they understand the value of those expectations. Before teachers make assignments and establish rules for conduct and classroom procedures, they should be certain these things are "doable" and worth student effort. See Form 6.1 for questions that need to be answered before teachers request specific student behaviors and set consequences for failure to comply.

Form 6.1 SHOULD I ASK STUDENTS TO DO THIS ASSIGNMENT OR DEMONSTRATE THIS BEHAVIOR?

1. Do students see the value of this assignment or behavior?
2. Can students successfully complete this work?
3. Have I established the value of this assignment or behavior in my own mind?
4. Am I giving this assignment to keep students quiet?
5. Am I giving this assignment because I am required to give homework?
6. Am I giving this assignment because students need to be punished?
7. Am I requiring this behavior because it makes me feel powerful?
8. Am I requiring this procedure because when I went to school I was required to do this?
9. What will this assignment accomplish?
10. Do students need the practice?

See if you can add some other questions to this list.

Effective managers make assignments and standards of behavior as attractive to students as possible. They create situations in which students are able to see the value of completing assignments and behaving appropriately. This makes "seeing to it" that students "do it" easier for teachers and more rewarding for students. Of course when a small number of students fail to comply, appropriate consequences must be given; but if almost all students fail to comply, then the value of the assignment or expectation should be questioned.

Some students may not be insightful or mature enough to realize the value of learning and behaving appropriately. When this happens external motivation must be used. Grades are powerful external motivation for many students. And because grades are common to almost all schools, effective managers make sure students understand the grading system.

HELPING STUDENTS UNDERSTAND A GRADING SYSTEM

Many students are motivated by grades. In fact, some students may be so concerned with grades that they ignore many of the important concepts and behaviors that should be learned in school but are not evaluated and graded. Most students know grades are important and want good grades, but many do not know what to do to get those good grades.

Effective classroom managers use a grading system students understand.

Many students at all grade levels, but especially in junior and senior high schools, are angered and frustrated by grades they believe are unfair. Anger is particularly prevalent if students do not understand how grades are determined. For example, Jeff is a tenth grade student with a history of low achievement. His records indicate he has average intelligence. English is his second language; he works after school and on weekends. Jeff realizes the economic importance of an education and wants to learn and get good grades. He likes social studies and is enrolled in a history class. Every two weeks the teacher assigns a report that requires students to write a biographical sketch of a person who influenced the events being studied in class. Jeff knows there is a penalty for late papers, but he doesn't understand how the penalty works. All the teacher has told the class is that papers are worth 25 points and that there is a penalty for late papers. Jeff likes doing the papers and thinks those he has completed are "pretty good," but each paper has been two or three days late. It is the end of a nine-week grading period, and three of Jeff's papers have not been graded and returned. The teacher has given two pop quizzes, and Jeff failed both of them; but he made a C+ on the nine-week test. He does not know that the two pop quizzes are worth 30 percent of his test score for the grading period. When he gets his report card Jeff receives a D-. He is angry and upset because he thought he would get no lower than a C and hoped for a B-. He decides it makes no difference if he "tries" or if he "goofs off." After he got his report card, he began skipping class, refused to participate in class, and has begun a friendship with a student who has behavior problems. The teacher's failure to keep Jeff informed of the evaluation of his written assignments and explain the grading system pushed Jeff to become an even lower achiever and, finally, a behavior problem.

Because grades are important to both low and high achieving students, the method of evaluating work and determining a grade should be communicated clearly in both oral and written form. A grading system, when understood by students, can prevent problem behavior, and motivate students to be aware of their progress and regulate their own effort and work habits.

Form 6.2 WHAT I DON'T LIKE ABOUT SCHOOL
___

IF i thank about it I get all upset.
SO I better
pass on this one today.
Thanks. No hard feelens.
what i donlike school—NO A
what i dont like school is that i come every day
thanking i will get a A. but I never get a A.
Just wonst I want to get a A. Ever sins I
remember I go to school a thousand day a
year or more I get no A. No A
JUST WONST I WANT AN A
ONE BIG FAT A
All I git is a gib funch of F
A hundred F. A thowsand F
A lowsy bunch of F

Author Unknown

___

From Discipline in Schools: A Source Book, North Carolina Department of Public Instruction, 1976, p. 75.

Many effective managers in junior and senior high schools help students understand their grades by determining the number of points possible for a student to earn in a grading period. They assign points for each student activity such as quizzes, projects, scheduled tests, written assignments, homework, and class participation. Some teachers give each student a written form that lists each activity and the points possible, and they require students to record their own grades. They periodically encourage students to compare points possible and the number the student has earned. When motivation to learn and earn points is low, some teachers give points for daily or weekly participation and record points on the student's score card. An effective grading system can also enhance desirable work habits by rewarding promptness in completing assignments with extra points. Extra points can be given for any behavior the teacher wants students to practice and thus make it possible for low achieving students to raise their grade as well as practice desirable work and study habits. In order for a grading system of any type to be effective, the teacher must also be prompt in evaluating students' work.

An effective grading system can help students understand that participation, attendance, daily work, completing assignments, and completing assignments on time affect a grade. It especially helps less motivated and low achieving students understand the consequences of daily effort and action (Sprick, 1985).

A grading system appropriately designed for a specific group of students and fully understood by those students reminds them of why they are in school, focuses their attention to learning, and will over time motivate them to develop the self-discipline to study and behave in appropriate ways.

Form 6.3 CHECKLIST FOR EVALUATING TEACHING SELF-DISCIPLINE

How did you teach self-discipline?

____ 1. By modeling self-discipline.
____ 2. By having students practice appropriate behavior.
____ 3. By recognizing progress made by students in learning self-discipline.
____ 4. By avoiding punishment and finding alternatives.
____ 5. By avoiding criticism.
____ 6. By using praise effectively.
____ 7. By avoiding confrontations with students.

____ 8. By using feedback to inform instead of to evaluate.
____ 9. By holding students accountable.
____ 10. By using a grading system that encourages students to "keep up" with their own achievement and behavior.

SUMMARY

Teachers who are credible, value learning, and care about and respect students can prevent many behavior problems. The ultimate goal, however, is to develop students' internal motivation to function as productive, social members of the classroom and the larger society—students who need little or no prodding, monitoring, or punishment to achieve academically and behave appropriately, students who are self-disciplined.

In this chapter some teacher behaviors that can help students learn to manage their own behavior in appropriate ways have been suggested. Effective managers teach students self-discipline by (1) modeling self-discipline, (2) making it possible for students to practice appropriate behavior, (3) avoiding using punishment and criticism, (4) finding alternatives to punishment, (5) avoiding teacher-student conflicts, (6) using feedback and praise in appropriate ways; (7) holding students accountable, and (8) making sure students understand the method of arriving at grades.

When these principles of effective management are used, students should make progress in developing behaviors that demonstrate self-control. Some of these behaviors are:

1. listening or keeping quiet when others are talking;
2. staying in seats and attending to task when the teacher steps out of sight;
3. completing assignments without constant reminders to do so;
4. speaking in calm voices to each other and the teacher;
5. following routines and procedures on their own;
6. setting goals for themselves and working toward those goals, for example, "I am going to earn an A this grading period;"
7. looking out for the welfare of others, for example, treating others the way they want to be treated;

8. expecting no special treatment;
9. accepting consequences for their behavior and not blaming others; and
10. contributing to the classroom group process in positive ways.

Sometimes teachers become frustrated and demoralized when students do not "learn to behave" immediately. A student teacher, who had been reminded by her supervisor to avoid criticism, consciously and successfully gave appropriate feedback and praise and avoided teacher-student conflicts and criticism for an entire day. The following day her students acted up and behaved terribly. She told her supervisor, "I was nice to them yesterday. Why aren't they good today?"

Teachers must be patient in teaching self-discipline and realistic in evaluating students' progress. Success is often realized in small behaviors that reflect changes in students' attitudes. Compare students' self-discipline in June with their behavior when they came to your classroom in September. If you practice the behaviors of effective managers, you may have been more successful than you think.

The next and final part of this book will continue to give suggestions for preventing behavior problems and teaching self-discipline. Chapter 7 is devoted to helping teachers plan for managing classrooms, teaching discipline, and involving parents. Chapter 8 summarizes and explains a philosophy of managing classrooms and teaching discipline.

QUESTIONS AND ACTIVITIES

6.1 If you are a student teacher or have a class of your own:
(a) Identify those students who have the most self-discipline. Make a list of their behaviors that led you to this conclusion.
(b) Identify those students who have the least self-discipline. Make a list of their behaviors that led you to this conclusion.
6.2 If you or a teacher you have observed have had a student-teacher confrontation, analyze how you or the teacher got drawn into this conflict. Make a plan that would have made it possible to avoid the situation.
6.3 Make a list of noncritical responses you can make to students who are behaving inappropriately.
6.4 Make a list of feedback statements that are not evaluative.

6.5 Make a list of statements that praise specifically. Practice using these phrases.

6.6 Make a list of students you "caught" behaving appropriately.

6.7 Choose one of the principles of teaching self-discipline discussed in this chapter and outline an approach you would use to implement this principle.

6.8 Think back to your own experiences. Describe an incident or a teaching method that helped you acquire self-discipline.

6.9 If you have ever been punished in a physical way, tell your reactions then and now.

6.10 What was the most effective punishment or consequence used with you? What are your thoughts about this punishment? Did it help you achieve self-discipline?

6.11 What does Haim Ginott mean when he says, "Punishment breeds sadistic or masochistic brutality?"

6.12 Make a list of problem behaviors to which teachers often respond with criticism. List some alternative teacher behaviors to criticism.

REFERENCES

Bandura, A. (1969). *Principles of Behavior Modification.* New York: Holt, Rinehart, and Winston.

Bandura, A. (1977). *Social Learning Theory.* Englewood Cliffs, N.J.: Prentice-Hall.

Brophy, J. (1979). *Teacher Praise: A Functional Analysis.* (Occasional paper No. 28.) East Lansing, Mich.: Michigan State University, Institute for Research on Teaching.

Brophy, J. (1981). "Teacher Praise: A Functional Analysis." *Review of Educational Research, 51,* pp. 5–32.

Curwin, R., and Mendler, A. (1988). "We Repeat, Let the Buyer Beware: A Response to Canter." *Educational Leadership, 46* (6), p. 83.

Dreikurs, R. (1971). *Maintaining Sanity in the Classroom: Illustrated Teaching Techniques.* New York: Harper and Row.

Etizioni, A. (1982a). "The Role of Self-Discipline." *Phi Delta Kappan, 63* (3), pp. 184–188.

Etizioni, A. (1982b). *An Immodest Agenda.* New York: McGraw-Hill.

Flanders, N. (1970). *Analyzing Teacher Behavior.* Reading, Mass.: Addison-Wesley.

Gartrell, D. (1987). "Punishment or Guidance?" *Young Children, 42* (3), pp. 55–61.

Ginott, H. (1972). *Between Teacher and Child.* New York: Macmillan, pp. 63–64, 147–152, 167–168.

Good, T., and Brophy, J. (1987). *Looking in Classrooms* (4th ed.). New York: Harper and Row, p. 269.

Gordon, T. (1974). *T.E.T. Teacher Effectiveness Training*. New York: Peter Wyden.

Hamilton, S. (1983). "Synthesis of Research on the Social Side of Schooling." *Educational Leadership, 40* (5), pp. 65–72.

Kounin, J. (1970). *Discipline and Group Management in Classrooms*. New York: Holt, Rinehart and Winston.

Landfried, S. (1988). "Talking to Kids about Things that Matter." *Educational Leadership, 45* (8), pp. 32–35.

McDaniel, T. (1986). "A Primer on Classroom Discipline." *Phi Delta Kappan, 68* (1), pp. 63–67.

North Carolina Department of Public Instruction (1976). *Discipline in Schools: A Source Book*. Raleigh, N.C.: North Carolina Department of Education, p. 75.

Pereira, C. (1988). "Educating for Citizenship in the Elementary Grades." *Phi Delta Kappan, 69* (6), pp. 429–432.

Sprick, R. S. (1985). *Discipline in the Secondary School*. West Nyack, N.J.: The Center for Applied Research in Education.

Four

GETTING IT ALL TOGETHER

*I*n Part One teacher characteristics essential for effective management and teaching self-discipline were identified. Part Two was devoted to preventing management and discipline problems. In Part Three suggestions were given for resolving problems, maintaining an effectively managed classroom, and teaching discipline.

Part Four addresses planning for behavior and involving parents and summarizes essentials for success in effectively managing classrooms and teaching discipline. In Chapter 7 planning for student behavior and involving parents is presented as fundamental to using all other principles of management and discipline and to creating the teacher's vision of his or her ideal classrooms. Chapter 8 is a summary of principles of effective management and teaching discipline—a summary with a philosophy.

Chapter
7

Planning for Behavior and Involving Parents

INTRODUCTION AND OBJECTIVES

Any discussion of essentials of classroom management and teaching discipline would be imperfectly conceived and falsely presented without giving special attention to planning for behavior problems and involving parents. These two dimensions of the educational enterprise underlie all other dimensions; without planning for behavior and without the cooperation of parents, we cannot realize that ideal classroom environment each of us envisions. Planning for behavior and involving parents illuminate the dimness and uncertainty of our classrooms; and if planning is not done and parents are not involved, any acceptable learning climate that flourishes by happenstance can be quickly snatched away and the joy of any success will be diminished because it does not extend to the students' total life. When teachers plan for behavior and involve parents, they can orchestrate successful student life in classrooms that enhances and extends to the home and society.

The purpose of this chapter is to emphasize and reemphasize the importance of planning for student behavior and involving parents. After you have completed this chapter you will be able to:

- give a rationale for making behavior plans,
- list and understand guidelines for planning for behavior,
- use guidelines to plan for students' behavior,

- list reasons for involving parents,
- plan a parent conference,
- explain "realistic" expectations of parents, and
- suggest ways to involve parents.

PLANNING FOR BEHAVIOR

It has already been said that after you have taught discipline, you can teach anything; and until you have taught discipline, nothing is learned. Everyone seems to recognize the importance of teaching discipline and academics. Both preservice teacher education and in-service staff development programs emphasize the importance of planning to teach academic content, but little is said about *planning* to teach discipline. The foci of most teacher training are (1) teaching planning for instruction that will interest students and prevent behavior problems; (2) organizing and managing materials, seating, and so on; (3) a few techniques from behavior modification programs; and (4) how to be assertive. These are all important. It is important to note, however, that the emphasis has been on "formal" written planning for teaching content and managing classrooms; little attention has been paid to thoughtful, comprehensive planning for behavior.

The importance of planning for managing classrooms and teaching discipline has been alluded to throughout this book. You have been told to plan to (1) acquire those attitudes and behaviors essential for effective classroom management and teaching discipline, (2) prevent management and behavior problems, (3) resolve behavior problems, (4) maintain an effectively managed classroom, and (5) teach self-discipline. Suggestions have been offered in terms of what to plan for, and in some instances guidelines for planning specific approaches have been given, for example, guidelines for using seatwork.

Many teachers say they plan in their heads, but this plan is often no more than a "gimmick" they plan to use. Some teachers plan for teaching the academics and simply hope that students will behave appropriately. Many classroom conditions call for a plan to teach curriculum content and a behavior plan to teach discipline, which will make it possible to teach the content. Instead of simply planning an interesting lesson (and this is necessary), a behavior plan for maintaining "good discipline" or for resolving any undesirable behavior should be developed. Planning for teaching content and planning for behavior may be done separately or in concert, but it must be done.

You have already been alerted to planning for seating, using materials, and so on, as ways of preventing problems. In addition, knowing the developmental levels of students can certainly give clues to planning for appropriate rules, pacing, level of difficulty, and so on. Regardless of one's preplanning and insight into the nature of students, problems will arise that need specific attention. When a few or many students do not attend to learning or display disruptive behavior, teachers can attend to and resolve these problems through careful, deliberate planning.

Effective Classroom Managers Make Behavior Plans for Specific Students in Specific Situations.

The first step in developing a behavior plan is to compile all possible data relative to the student or group for which the plan is being made. One way to synthesize the data is to write a description of the students' behavior and the classroom situation. Be sure to include everything you know about the students and the classroom atmosphere. You should also state your feelings about the students and their behavior. (See Form 7.1.)

Form 7.1 DATA NEEDED TO PLAN FOR STUDENTS' BEHAVIOR

1. What is the age of the student?
2. What is the achievement level of the student?
3. What is the socioeconomic status of the student?
4. Who are the student's friends?
5. What are the student's interests?
6. What happens before the behavior occurs (include teacher behavior)?
7. What happens after the behavior occurs (include teacher behavior)?
8. What classroom activity is in progress when the behavior occurs?
9. What time of day does the behavior occur?
10. What does the student do after the behavior occurs?
11. Other?
12. How do you feel about the student?
13. What are the student's strengths?

The next step is to analyze the data and look for possible reasons why these students are misbehaving. Be aware of two cautions. First, teachers are not psychiatrists; therefore, be wary of attributing motives for the behavior. Your conclusions may not be valid and may damage your relationship with the students as well as prevent finding a relatively simple solution to the problem. Second, ask yourself if the general classroom atmosphere and your attitude and behavior contribute to, if not cause, the behavior. Remember, when many students frequently misbehave something is amiss in the learning environment. Do not dismiss your own behavior as being appropriate in all situations. After you have hypothesized possible reasons for the problems, set a goal or goals and develop a behavior plan for students, the teacher, or the students and teacher.

Behavior plans can focus on resolving a specific problem behavior, teaching discipline, maintaining a desirable learning climate, eliminating or instilling a behavior or attitude, and increasing a desirable behavior or attitudes. It can be designed for the teacher, one student, a few students, or an entire group. Behavior plans have the same essential components as lesson plans—objectives, procedures, and a method for evaluating the effectiveness of the procedures. A behavior plan reflects what the teacher will or will not do to help students acquire self–discipline. A summary of these components follows.

1. A behavior plan should have a long–range goal.
2. A behavior plan should have a short–range goal.
3. A behavior plan should have procedures for accomplishing long– and short–range goals.
4. A behavior plan must have a way of determining the effectiveness of the procedures, for example, a test or observations of behavior.
5. All planning for behavior must be based on student levels of behavior, and so you must know something about students.

Many teachers resist lesson planning as unnecessary, and many teachers will resist making behavior plans for the same reasons; however, thoughtful, well–conceived, and well–executed behavior plans can make a dramatic difference in student behavior.

The importance of classroom management and discipline was discussed by a group of first–year middle, junior, and senior high school teachers who attended a workshop on managing classrooms and teaching discipline. The workshop, part of an alternative teacher certification program, was conducted over a period of six Saturdays. The group members had been teaching since August; the workshop was conducted in December and January. The sole criterion for selection of the participants was a desire to secure certification, not their ability or lack of ability to manage a classroom or to teach discipline. Several members of the group described student behavior in their classrooms as good or excellent. Others expressed dismay at the lack of their students' self–control and their own ability to manage a classroom. Some were ready to "give up"; others were skeptical of the effectiveness of an "education workshop"; still others were "willing to try anything." After discussion of essential teacher characteristics, writing and enforcing rules and procedures, getting to know students, and other points, the workshop instructor gave these teachers the following instructions:

Assignment

Choose a behavior displayed by your total class, part of the group, or an individual student. Develop a plan to resolve the problem and teach discipline. Your plan should have:

1. Long–range goal(s).
2. Short–range goal(s) (daily or weekly).
3. Procedure(s).
4. Method(s) of checking for success.

When you have finished you will have a strategy for preventing or resolving one kind of disruptive behavior. Somewhere in this plan you should tell what you know about students, your observations, your conclusions. Try your plan for a minimum period of one week, and evaluate the results. You may want to make some changes in your strategy.

Some examples of the plans that were developed are quoted with permission. Note that each plan is based on a thoughtful analysis of the behavior problem. The first is an example of planning for a total class.

PLAN ONE

Background:

I developed this classroom management plan for my sixth period pre-algebra course. These are my least motivated, most disruptive students of the day. They are my only nonhonors course. They are the ninth grade students that are taking the lowest math possible without being classified as LD or EH. I am challenged by this class because of their needs; yet it is sixth period for them and for me, and it shows in all of us. This is also a large class of 36 students. Throughout the year I have been changing strategies constantly to improve the horrible beginning. I have reached a point where everyone is doing their classwork because I am giving them daily grades. The discipline is still not satisfactory. This class of students especially wants to be my friends. They like to ask my opinion on matters, discuss out-of-school topics, and sometimes just chat. I want to be their friend and teacher. They are at an age where this is important. It is just a hard role to fill.

Long-Range Goals:

I am an optimist, but I would like to see this class sit quietly while I lecture, work independently of each other, and study for quizzes and tests. I would like for the grades to be distributed in the A, B, and high C range instead of the current low C, D and F range. I would like them to be interested in moving up to algebra next year in high school and feel prepared for it. I feel they are capable of all these things and would like to pull them out.

Short-Range Goals:

I tackle *one* discipline problem at a time. This week's goal was to have the students come to class prepared. The most often forgotten material happens to be their textbook. My goal was to have them bring their books every day. This will make them feel more serious in class, but it will also help them to be organized in other aspects of classroom living. This will also prevent the sharing of textbooks and keep the noise level low. This week I work on materials; next week maybe I can emphasize staying in seats.

Procedures and Observations:

Monday:

The class was presented our new policy in the following way: I will check for materials each day. If you do not have your textbook, you will receive an F in the gradebook. But at the end of the grading period, if you have brought your materials every day, you will receive a quiz grade of A.

One student who did not have her textbook asked, "Does this start today?" I was excited about her concern. I told them I would start checking tomorrow. They were reminded again of our new policy before they left class.

Tuesday:

After conducting today's lesson and assigning classwork, I walked around the room with gradebook in hand to check for textbooks, and to my surprise, only two students were bookless. These two students were reminded of the rule, while the other students were congratulated on their effort.

Wednesday:

When checking for books today, I found two other students without their books. One student had a covered science book and claimed he had picked up the wrong book from his locker. He asked permission to change it. The other student said she had gone to her locker before class and was not allowed to open it due to the new locker schedule. She also requested to go to her locker. Both students were permitted to go in order to show trust in their reasons, but warned not to repeat the same mistakes. The class was reminded of their potential As at the end of nine weeks.

Thursday:

I was unable to observe due to an absence.

Friday:

When checking for books on Friday, I had four students without texts. The locker schedule was blamed for most of them, but this time they were *not* permitted to get their texts. I feel that this did have something to do with the locker schedule because this day administration was enforcing it strongly, but I also feel it had to do with my absence yesterday. The students probably did not expect me to return to class today.

The four students were given Fs and one remarked, "There goes my quiz A."

Conclusions:

I have found that any plan seems to work better than expected when extra effort is used. I seem to be the key to all discipline. If I am consistent with my rules—which I admit I am not always—the students react as desired. I was concentrating on this project and enforcing the rule, and it showed in the students' behavior. They seemed concerned about their grades, and I noticed increased effort in bringing materials with little work on my part except for my attention to the problem. My main goal is consistency. I have to display this with every rule and my work will be smoother.

Notice that the short–range goal of having students come to class prepared was partially achieved through consistent application of the procedure used. This teacher appears to have discovered the importance of consistency and made a successful first step toward changing her behavior as well as that of students. She should continue to work toward this first goal and, when appropriate, choose another disruptive behavior and develop a procedure for eliminating it.

The second teacher plans to prevent four students with behavior problems from disrupting a well–managed classroom.

PLAN TWO

Background:

The student group I work with is composed of sixth graders. Four are new to my classroom because of reorganization. This plan is for those four students. I was told by various teachers that the change in students was not in my favor. Teachers being teachers, I had nightmare stories being told to me about this new group. Well, I decided I would be ready for them. I envisioned myself with my guns strapped to my legs ready for the shootout at the OK Corral!

1. Student A: minority student, lower socioeconomic scale, labeled LD or EH.
2. Student B: minority student, lower socioeconomic scale, a flasher!

3. Student C: minority student, lower socioeconomic scale, mover and talker.
4. Student D: minority student, lower socioeconomic scale, mover and talker.

Long-Range Goal:

My long-range goal is to keep these students from interrupting my class and bothering fellow students by talking and moving around.

Short-Range Goal:

My short-range goal is to keep them within my immediate viewing range and working. I hope this will alleviate their off-task behavior. My first concern was to let them know the rules and exactly what I expected from them.

Day 1:

The procedures I have followed so far are: as soon as these individuals came into class, I had them sit in the front seats across the first four rows. This meant I would have them within an arm's reach at all times.

After I had them seated along with the rest of the class, I went over the class rules. I had all students read the rules, and we discussed them. I also had new students write the rules and sign them, stating that they understood. I used the same five rules I had been using in my classes, but this time around I am trying to use consistency, which to this point has been my weakness!

I assigned special chores for the four boys I am concerned with. They have to come in and immediately get the textbooks for their rows and collect them. This allows them to move, but in a productive instead of a disruptive manner.

Days 2 Through 5:

I have reinforced these rules every day by reviewing them and implementing them. I have also used a lot of praise when these students are performing in a desired fashion.

Observations From Week and Conclusions:

I have had a lot of success. By using this seating arrangement to control their activities and putting demands on them, they have less time to be disruptive. So far they are producing satisfactory work and their outbursts have been minimal.

Notice this teacher plans for seating, teaching and enforcing rules, and getting the students to participate in positive ways.

A third teacher's plan is designed to help one student acquire some self-discipline.

PLAN THREE

Background:

Cabot is a problem in my Spanish class. He's an eighth-grader with a few emotional/psychological problems, but in general, he is a good kid. The problem I have with Cabot is that he's extremely impatient. The slightest comment another student makes that doesn't appeal to Cabot or anything that happens which Cabot finds annoying, he bursts out with, "Shut up," or "You're a jerk." If not those comments, then something to that effect. This might actually seem like a halfway normal reaction from a thirteen-year-old, but the intensity of his comments is very disturbing not only to me, but also to his fellow students. Conducting this class successfully is not an easy job. Since Cabot is very impatient and if he doesn't under-stand some aspect of Spanish grammar, or if he gets a bad grade on an assignment, he will say, "This is stupid. Why do they talk like that any-way?" Or he might ball-up a quiz he is in the middle of taking and refuse to do the work.

Procedures:

I've spoken with his mother and his counselor, and both have conveyed to me different emotional situations that he's going through. Behavior such as this, though, cannot be excused. This undesirable behavior has con-tinued long after parent-teacher meetings. I decided to try to modify Cabot's behavior myself.

Obviously, my long-range goal was to instill some patience into the student and to let him realize patience can be important. I also wanted him to open up to the other students in order for the others not to think of him as "strange" or "mean."

I realized the best thing to do would be to set up a series of short-range goals that Cabot could easily achieve within a short period of time. The first goal was to somehow get Cabot to pay more attention. Since it was the beginning of a new semester, this was fairly easy to achieve. The new semester meant new seating arrangements. I moved Cabot closer to the front, where he would receive less distractions. It seemed to help. Five minutes after being moved, he asked a very logical and intelligent grammar question.

I somehow had to control his outbursts when something bothered him. That problem didn't go away by moving him to the front. One of the other students asked a question because she was a little confused. Cabot turned around and said "God, you're stupid!" So, in a little more exaggerated tone than Cabot used, I turned to the same girl and said, "God, you're stupid!" She smiled. Cabot knew what I was doing, and there were no more outbursts that day. The next objective would be to make sure that there would not be any "bratty" behavior the next day.

As soon as I saw Cabot the next day, I made a special point to talk to him alone—find out how he was doing and if he was ready to work. Of course, he said he wasn't ready and that he did not do his homework. I told him I was disappointed but that he still could do well that day. He told me, "I'll try," which was progress.

Conclusions:

I have had only two weeks to employ this strategy. I have already seen marked improvement in Cabot's attitude and behavior. The other students are not excluding him as much anymore because of his new attitude. I was also able to evaluate the success of my first attempt at behavior change by looking at Cabot's behavior and the attitudes of others towards him and his behavior at the end of the two weeks. The other students are accepting him more, and he isn't complaining as much anymore. He is even taking criticism. All this in such a short time seems, for me, almost impossible. I doubt this *all* came about because of me. I am happy to report, though, he is doing homework, classwork and doing well on quizzes.

Although this plan is not as specifically stated as the previous ones, it is fairly clear what was expected and what was done. In this case, one of the most important outcomes was that the teacher felt she had the ability to intervene in a positive way in this student's behavior. (See Form 7.2.)

Form 7.2 GUIDELINES FOR BEHAVIOR PLANS

1. Identify the problem behavior and the students involved.
2. Decide what you would like changed over a period of time. Write long-range goal(s).
3. Use your knowledge of students' interests and their levels of cognitive, physical, moral, and social development, and write procedures for accomplishing your goals.
4. Devise way(s) to determine if your procedures are effective, for example, tests, observations, projects, conferences with student(s) and parents.
5. Try your plan. If you see signs of success, continue. If you meet with little or no success, make another plan. You may need to have "smaller" step-by-step goals or you may need different or more consistent application of procedures.
6. Give your plan time to work before you abandon it. Neither Rome nor discipline is built in a day.

Another teacher used a simple form of reinforcement to diminish tardiness in a ninth grade Basic Skills Mathematics class.

PLAN FOUR

Background:

Students in the Basic Skills Mathematics class are grade conscious; however, they are accustomed to receiving poor grades. They need immediate feedback and rewards for their effort. Eighty percent arrive late for class.

Long- and Short-Range Goal:

To diminish tardiness.

Procedures:

Each day on-time students are rewarded with some sort of grade enhancement. To achieve my goal I must begin class on time and reward on-time students consistently on a daily basis: (1) on-time students receive three points; (2) students who return homework on time receive three points. At the end of the week each student can earn 30 points, which are added to the cumulative score, and students are informed of their total scores each week.

Conclusions:

At the end of a nine-week grade period only two students continue to be tardy on a regular basis.

All members of this workshop who developed clearly thought out plans and consistently used the procedures indicated that progress was made in resolving or preventing the behavior problem. Of course, persistent and consistent application of procedures must be continued. Other problems will also have to be planned for and resolved before student behavior meets a desirable standard.

In Chapter 6 it was suggested that students must understand the system used to determine their grade, and it was also suggested that systematic awarding of points for a desired behavior, such as raising hands before answering, can help students learn self-discipline. The following is a plan developed by a middle school teacher for awarding points to increase student participation. Notice the systematic, carefully thought out goals and procedures he conveys to students. Also note the use of behavior contracting, as suggested in Chapter 6.

PLAN FIVE

Background:

The students in fifth period physical science class are not well disciplined. They call out, are late to class, are apathetic, and generally show low achievement. It is difficult but not yet impossible to teach this group of students.

Long-Range Goal:

The students will improve their conduct and academic grades by acquiring points for class participation.

Short-Range Goal:

The students will be able to explain the use of points for class participation and begin to work to earn points.

Procedures:

(1) A point system for class participation will be introduced to the students. (2) Each student will receive a copy of the plan, which they will sign and return the signature sheet to the teacher. (3) A chart of the point system will be posted in the classroom, and the total number of points for each activity and each student will be posted at the end of each week or at the beginning of the following week.

RULES AND GUIDELINES
for
MIDDLE SCHOOL PHYSICAL SCIENCE CLASSES
CLASS PARTICIPATION GRADE

In each nine-week grading period we have 45 days of school. On each of these days you start with 5 points. You may lose points for breaking any of the following rules or for any other item listed below.

The rules are:

1. Follow directions the first time they are given.
2. Be in class, seated, and quiet when the bell rings.
3. Bring books, notebooks, pens, and pencils to class *every day*.
4. Raise hand to be recognized before speaking.
5. Keep hands, feet, and objects to yourself.
6. Teacher dismisses class, *not the bell*. (Wait for teacher dismissal.)

Other Behaviors:

If the teacher finds it necessary *to remind you* about any of the above rules, you lose one (1) point for each reminder except in the case of tardiness.

If you are tardy to class, you lose two (2) points, and if you are absent, you lose four (4) points. However, if your absence is for a valid reason, you may make up the work and earn back your lost points. The work must be made up immediately upon return to class unless you make other arrangements with the teacher.

The total number of points possible for the nine weeks is 225. This will become a letter grade which counts as 10 percent of your final grade. The letter grade will be obtained by following the schedule below:

SCALE:

> 203–225 = A
> 180–202 = B
> 158–179 = C
> 135–157 = D
> 134 & BELOW = F

YOUR FINAL GRADE WILL BE DETERMINED AS FOLLOWS:

TEST GRADES	60%
QUIZZES	10%
HOME/CLASS WORK	20%
CLASS PARTICIPATION	_10%_
TOTAL	100%

Notebooks will be graded and count as one test grade. The weekly points will be listed on a poster or other such thing on the wall of the room. The totals will be posted on Friday at the end of class or on Monday before class. There is a possibility that the person with the highest number of points and the person with the greatest improvement will receive some sort of prize!

Also if the entire class does well, we may see a movie before a holiday or teacher workday!

I, _____, have read and understand the rules for class participation and conduct and guidelines for earning points.

_____   _____
Date   Signature

First Day Lesson Plan

Objective:

The student will understand and be able to explain the behavior and academic plan that will be introduced.

Procedures:

(1) The teacher will hand out the copies of the new class participation plan. See below. (2) Through a student/teacher question/answer session, the rules and methods will be explained. (3) Examples of the types of unacceptable participation will be given, such as yelling out answers, being tardy to call, and so on. (4) Seatwork assignment is to read and sign the plan and return the signature sheet to the teacher.

Evaluation:

The teacher will observe and determine by random questioning if understanding has been achieved.

Follow-Up Plans:

The teacher must be consistent in using the point system. This will take special effort and time. If it works it will be worth it.

General Comments:

Although the behavioral plan was originally set up to handle the discipline problems in my fifth period class, I initiated the plan in all of my classes. I found that it made quite a difference even in the first week.

The plan was introduced to the students on a Monday and implemented on Tuesday. An immediate improvement was visible in my classes that were basically under control; however, the class for which the plan was originated took longer to show improvement.

My fifth period class finally began to respond on Friday, and I was actually able to have meaningful academic learning time for the first time in a very long time. Perhaps over time the plan will work for a larger number of the students with discipline problems.

The final example of a behavior plan was made by a preservice teacher. Notice the succinctness and clarity of the plan. The student was unable to implement the plan due to his university class schedules. Do you think it would work?

PLAN SIX

Problem:

Currently the band members enter the room loudly and do not immediately take their seats. Approximately ten minutes are lost at the beginning of every period because they do not know how to get started.

Long-Range Goal:

The band will enter quietly, and a student conductor will warm up the band. Five minutes after the bell rings, the instructor will give the first downbeat, and everybody will be there to see it.

Short-Range Goals:

1. Have student section leaders take charge.
2. Have students enter quietly.
3. Each week eliminate two minutes of the ten minute lag time.
4. Have one student per week warm up the band.

Procedures:

1. One student will stand outside the door to make sure that all enter quietly.
2. Section leaders will insure that all have their instruments and are in their seats after only three minutes.
3. The student conductor for the week will be in charge of the section leaders and will make sure they are moving quickly.
4. The student will begin warming up the band after three and a half minutes (approximately) or when the band is ready. He will try to keep to the schedule.
5. The section that is in their seats first will win quality points for the day. These points will go to decide which section will get to perform at the next concert.
6. Each day the band is in their seats on time, the whole group gets quality points.

Methods for Checking Success

1. I will check the time every day by starting and stopping the "band stopwatch." It is a smaller version of the ones used at swim meets. The dial is big enough for everybody to see.
2. The band will be made aware of my weekly goal—two minutes off each week.
3. I will make sure that quality points mean something. They will have a goal of a certain number of points. These points will be displayed on the bulletin board. They will know where they stand at all times.

Making a behavior plan does not ensure the resolution or prevention of problem behavior. After any plan is made it must be consciously and consistently implemented, and indeed it may not work because the goals or procedures may not be appropriate for this particular problem. If a behavior plan is implemented and fails to achieve the desired goals, try another approach. Planning for preventing and resolving behavior problems forces teachers to analyze situations, set goals, develop procedures, and evaluate what was done. Planning and executing behavior plans encourages teachers to do more than cross their fingers and hope students will behave. Remember, planning for behavior is equally as important as planning for academics. If you are currently teaching, use the suggested principles and guidelines and develop a behavior and discipline plan for your total student group, a small student group, or one student.

PLANNING FOR INVOLVING PARENTS

Let Me Be There

i
pay
you
to teach,
to administer,
to watch over
my children.

if
my children
disrupt
your class
or discover
the world,
tell me.[1]

---

[1]From *Discipline in Schools: A Source Book*, North Carolina Department of Public Instruction, 1976, p. 97.

Parents are children's first teachers, and the home is a child's first learning environment. It is the home that provides experiences that determine self-concept, values, attitudes, and readiness for schooling in academics and socialization. When parents enroll their children in schools, they entrust them to the care of teachers and acquire partners to educate their offspring. Contrary to some teachers' perceptions, most parents do not abdicate their responsibility for their child's education when the child goes to school. Parents expect to continue in the role of helping their children learn and behave, and they expect to be involved with and be a part of the education programs provided by the schools.

Some teachers perceive that parents "don't care enough" about their child or that they are too busy or simply unwilling to become involved with resolving inappropriate behavior or academic problems. As a result of this perception, teachers do not attempt to involve parents. They simply decry the students' home conditions and assume that parents either will not or cannot be helpful. It may be true that many parents are very busy and appear to resent the need to spend time working with their children's teachers. It may also be true that many parents are often reluctant to become involved with the school, because they feel powerless and have their own perceptions such as, "The schools are really not interested in my children, and teachers only give us a hard time and criticize." These perceptions of some teachers and parents can prevent both groups from making an effort to resolve problems through cooperation.

Effective Classroom Managers Let Parents Know the Need for Their Support and Plan for Involving Them in Resolving Behavior Problems.

Many teachers try to involve parents in a wide range of activities; other teachers avoid involving parents except perhaps when students have a major behavior problem. A growing body of research indicates that involving parents in their children's schooling improves achievement; and when children of all ages experience success, they are less likely to be behavior problems. Research studies also indicate that

. . . children from minority and low income families benefit most from parental involvement and parents do not have to be well educated to make a difference (Henderson, 1988.)

One research study (Berliner, 1985) indicates that teachers rarely contact parents of low–achieving students for the positive purpose of creating a "partnership for educating a child." Contact is usually made for attendance or behavior problems. The study showed, however, that in spite of this approach, when parents of low achievers were contacted, they did or tried to do what the teachers asked. Parents appeared interested and willing to be involved; the problem seems to not be with them, but with getting teachers to involve parents, especially in a positive fashion.

There are many ways to involve parents in schooling, such as serving on policymaking committees, serving as teachers' aides, planning and assisting with special progrmas, monitoring students' work or activities, and developing curriculum materials. The two most frequent kinds of involvement are helping with homework and conferencing with teachers in regard to achievement or behavior problems. When teachers need and want parents to help students with their academic homework or behavior problems, guidelines for helping should be communicated through writing, conferences, or phone calls. Standard homework and behavior policies should be written and sent to all parents. The most effective parental assistance is done in concert with the teacher's knowledge, planning, and cooperation.

In most schools parents expect to assist their children with school, and teachers expect them to assist. Some teachers expect parents to help them manage student behavior at school, teach students self–discipline, and resolve problems. Some teachers even expect that, once parents have been informed of their child's problem behavior, the parents will resolve the problem. Teachers must remember *they* are responsible for *classroom* behavior; the parents are not. Parents are informed of student behavior because they have a right to know and because they know more about their child than the teachers do. This knowledge, when combined with the teacher's knowledge, increases the possibility of the resolution of problems. Cooperation between parents and teachers increases the possibilities for attaining educational goals.

Contacting Parents about Behavior Problems

First contacts with parents should be positive. Many teachers make no effort to contact parents with good news and wait until there is a problem. As a result, the first personal contact is generally a phone call or a note, which often simplifies or magnifies the problem. In some school systems notes and phone calls to parents are routine procedures recommended or even mandated as part of the discipline program. For example, if a student has a serious behavior problem, the parents are called immediately. If the problem is not considered serious, second or third offenses may occur before parents are contacted. When school size and teacher–pupil ratios are considered, it is not surprising that these methods are used; however, there are more appropriate ways to contact parents which motivate all parties—teachers, parents, and students—to establish communication and resolve problems.

One teacher's formula for success is:

> Never criticize a student unless you are face to face with the parent. It is foolish to phone to make a complaint because you have no way of knowing what is happening at the other end of the line, and the phone is a useless tool for resolving problems. I want parents to look me in the eye when they tell me about their child, and I want to look them in the eye so they can see I am truly concerned and want to help their child.

Another teacher says:

> Few persons can communicate in writing the reasons for student failure or conduct. I do not want to communicate about such serious problems on some lifeless administrative form.

Another teacher says he says something good about a student before he makes any suggestions for improvement, and

> . . . if I can't think of some desirable attribute or behavior, I have no business calling or writing a note because this means I don't know enough about that student.

If your school district has a specified procedure for calling parents in regard to behavior problems, try to make a positive contact by phone, written communication, or conference before behavior problems arise. A positive phone call or note from a secondary teacher can be just as important to parents and students as one from the kindergarten teacher.

Conferencing

Many schools also require teachers to conduct parent–teacher conferences routinely. The purpose is for parents and teachers to know each other and develop effective lines of communication.

In a study of parent–school communication Lindle (1989) interviewed parents, principals, and teachers to identify methods used by schools to promote communication between the school and the home. She found that parents gave routine conferences poor ratings primarily because of the limited time and the formality. Lindle's study revealed that school personnel believe a professional, businesslike approach to talking with parents earns respect, but parents see "professionalism" as "too businesslike," too "patronizing," or as "talking down." Parents liked the personal touch

> . . . which means timely information on an informal basis is most likely to win parents' esteem.

Lindle also found that parent–teacher

> . . . disagreements increased with seniority, training, and formality of the teacher.

And the socioeconomic status of the parents did not affect their preferences about the nature of communications with the school. Parents indicated they appreciate teachers who take their work schedules into account when they schedule conferences. One parent said, "Conferences should be saved for big things." In spite of the fact that many parents do not like routine conferences, if they are will planned and conducted appropriately, they can be effective in enlisting parental support for partnerships and resolving problems. (See Form 7.3.)

Form 7.3 SUGGESTIONS FOR PARENT CONFERENCES

1. You might want to make a little sign for your door such as, "In conference. Please do not disturb."
2. Have the child's work in his or her folder and readily available as you discuss his or her progress.
3. Display some of the books you are using for the child's classwork. Parents are interested in seeing these.
4. Conduct the conference in an attractive setting, whether at the reading table or around your desk.
5. Be sure to do a lot of *listening*.
6. Be friendly. Some parents are shy with teachers. If you are informal and relaxed, it will help the situation in such cases.

7. Conduct each conference privately and treat all information as confidential.
8. Many parents want to know how they can help their children at home. It is a good idea to be able to provide them with some ideas and suggestions for their particular child. This should be something the parent can do successfully and without complicated teaching procedures. Flash cards, work lists, practice workbooks, and other such materials fit into this category.
9. Tell the child's good points first. Help parents realize that although the child may be weak in one area, he or she may be strong in another. This can include citizenship, social adjustment, handwriting, creative writing, or addition.
10. Welcome parents' suggestions as to how you can work together to help the child.
11. Be realistic. Don't over-rate the child. Also, when you feel that parents are over-anxious to the point of pushing the child beyond his or her ability, be sure to make them aware of the damage this attitude may do.
12. Be honest. Discuss the child's level of achievement and behavior and the efforts being made to provide a good program for the child.
13. If you have time, it is a good idea to make notes following conferences (before you forget) in order to follow through on any suggestions or information that may be of help to you in working with the child. It will also help you to remember and keep any promises you may have made with regard to your plans in your classroom work with the individual child in question.
14. Finally, end the conference with an optimistic attitude and establish the feeling that you, as well as they, are sincerely interested in the child's welfare.

When a conference is scheduled routinely or for a specific problem, the teacher should establish specific goals for the conference. If the conference is routine, the goal may be to inform the parents about their child's work or to meet parents. If the conference is part of resolving a problem, the problem has to be clearly defined by the teacher, and the parents must be allowed to state the problem as they see it. Essential to successful conferencing is teachers who *listen* to parents. Even when parents' perceptions and views appear inaccurate, voicing their opinions will lead to strengthening the communication process. Too often teachers inform parents of their view of the problem and their expectations of parents and their children without listening. This produces alienation, not involvement. (See Form 7.4.)

Expectations of Parents and Teachers

Effective managers expect parents to be involved in their children's schooling in positive ways as well as to assist with resolving problems. Effective managers look for reasons for and plan to make positive contact with parents; they avoid making negative contacts when pos-

Form 7.4 PARENTS EXPECT TEACHERS TO:

1. Keep them informed about students' problem behavior before it becomes serious.
2. Be honest about students' academic progress and behavior.
3. Allow them to be part of problem resolution.
4. Be interested in parents enough to talk with them about their children.
5. Arrange conferences at a time when parents can participate.
6. Know students well enough to identify some good points.
7. Recognize that parents care about their children.

sible. They expect parents to help resolve students' problems, not "take care of the problem." Classroom behavior is the responsibility of the classroom teacher; behavior at home is the responsibility of the parents. Both teachers and parents should remember that a child should not have two standards of behavior. Remember, the ultimate goal of all—teachers, parents, and students—is self-discipline and social and academic achievement, which facilitates productive living in a democratic society. Teachers should encourage and use all the help they can get from those who have the same goals. (See Form 7.5.)

Form 7.5 TEACHERS EXPECT PARENTS TO:

1. Support school policy.
2. Assist students at home.
3. Provide information when requested.
4. Make an effort to know their children's teachers.
5. Make an effort to attend conferences.
6. Be a part of problem resolution.
7. Make an effect to facilitate attendance and deter tardiness.

Parents expect to be involved in their children's schooling and want the experience to be positive if possible. They expect teachers to keep them informed of their children's progress and behavior. They expect teachers to confide in them their children's successes and setbacks, and they expect honesty. If teachers suspect drug abuse or other serious problems, parents should be alerted to a possible problem. Both students and parents may deny the situation, but parents expect teachers to be honest even though it can be painful. Talking with parents about a behavior problem can be an extremely difficult and delicate matter. Discussing the behavior of one's child with a "stranger," even in a dispassionate way, is often so traumatic for parents that teachers are reluctant to be totally honest; as a result, parents often are protected from knowledge of the seriousness of the problem and fail to deal with it in appropriate ways. Parents also expect teachers to recognize they care about their children and want to help resolve any problems that arise.

Form 7.6 RESOURCES FOR INVOLVING PARENTS AND STUDENTS

1. Action for Children's Television (ACT), 20 University Road, Cambridge, MA 02138
2. Center for Early Adolescence, University of North Carolina at Chapel Hill, Suite 233, Carr Mill Mall, Carrboro, NC 27510
3. Center on Parent Involvement, Johns Hopkins University, c/o Joyce Epstein, 3505 North Charles Street, Baltimore, MD 21218
4. Children's Defense Fund (CDF), 122 C Street NW, Washington, DC 20001
5. Home and School Institute, 1201 16th Street NW, Washington, DC 20036
6. Just Say No Clubs, c/o Oakland Parents in Action, 1404 Franklin Street, Suite 610, Oakland, CA 94612
7. National Coalition for Parent Involvement in Education, 119 North Payne Street, Alexandria, VA 22314
8. National Committee on Youth Suicide Prevention, 67 Irving Place South, New York, NY 10003
9. National Congress of Parents and Teachers, 1201 16th Street NW, #619, Washington, DC 20036
10. Work and Family Research Council, The Conference Board, Inc., 845 Third Avenue, New York, NY 10022

SUMMARY

Planning to prevent behavior problems, resolve problems, and teach discipline has been emphasized throughout this text. Planning to manage behavior and teach discipline is every bit as important to teaching and learning as planning to teach reading, chemistry, or art; and effective managers plan for behavior as carefully and systematically as they plan for academics. The truth is that most teachers may know more about how to teach their subject and skills than they know about teaching discipline and managing classrooms; therefore, they should give special attention to planning for students' behavior and their own actions. Effective managers realize that preventing and resolving behavior problems and teaching discipline require setting behavior goals, selecting procedures for implementing those goals and evaluating progress. They plan to create the kind of classroom climate that enhances teaching and learning and nourishes students' self–esteem as well as their own. In this chapter specific guidelines for planning for behavior and examples of behavior plans have been suggested.

In addition, it has been stated that no approach to managing classrooms and teaching discipline is complete unless parents are involved. Parents and teachers must plan and work together to provide conditions that allow students to grow and achieve full academic and social competency. Effective managers plan to involve parents in students' schooling in positive ways. They do not wait until there is a behavior problem before contacting parents. They plan parent conferences to communicate significant information and the expectation that parents will participate in helping teachers help their children.

Chapter 8 will reiterate and summarize all the principles of successfully managing classrooms and teaching discipline discussed throughout this book.

QUESTIONS AND ACTIVITIES

7.1. The following descriptions of classroom situations were written by experienced teachers. Read each problem and, using the guidelines for planning in this chapter, write a behavior plan for each problem. For each group, if you were to assume the responsibility of teaching, what would you do, if anything, to change the climate?

(a) This is a Spanish class for native speakers which focuses on Spanish literature and grammar. The class is composed of students with a wide variation in ability to read and write Spanish. One student is the clown of the class. He does anything to get other students' attention and asks a question every five minutes of the teacher. If the teacher suggests the student find an answer himself, such as find the meaning of a word in the dictionary, he says things like, "That's your job," "You're not a good teacher," and "You don't know how to teach." When he comes to the pencil sharpener at the front of the room he makes faces at other students. He never works in class. The teacher has talked with the student's mother and got no help from her. She has referred him to his group counselor, and he told her, "My teacher is not a good teacher. I don't understand the class. I don't speak Spanish."

(b)This is a fourth grade class of 35 students. Four are gifted, 6 are working at first and second grade levels, and the remaining 25 vary in achievement from third grade to sixth grade levels. The teacher has little control in the classroom. Students listen only when they choose. They tell the teacher when it is time for lunch. There is a lot of talking and getting out of seats, but the noise is never loud enough to disturb other classes. The teacher sits at a table and teaches small groups. The only time she attempts to talk with the total class is to prepare to show a video. Homework is assigned but not done and not collected. Grades are high, students say they like the teacher, and there are few aggressive acts by students. Parents who have visited the classroom have never questioned the quality of instruction or discipline.

7.2. Make a behavior plan for resolving the following problem, described by a beginning teacher, and then outline a plan for a conference with the parents of the student.

I have one definite behavior problem in my classroom, a female in first period; and every day we lock horns. She is what we would call a "smartmouth" and wants attention. If I said, "Go jump off a two–story building," she would want to go off a five–story place. Yesterday she was passing food in the class. In a very quiet voice I said, "You know the rules and the consequences." She proceeded to look me right in the eye and stuff her face.

7.3. If you are teaching or observing others teach, choose a student whose parents need to be informed of his or her behavior. Develop a plan to inform the parents.

7.4. What are the advantages and disadvantages of using the phone to talk with parents?

7.5. When should parent conferences be called by teachers?

7.6. Write for information from at least one source listed on Form 7.6.

REFERENCES

Becher, R. (1984). *Parent Involvement: A Review of Research and Principles of Successful Practice*. Washington, D.C.: National Institute of Education.

Berliner, D. (1985). "Is Parent Involvement Worth the Effort?" *Instructor*, XCV, pp. 20–21.

Boyer, E. (1989). "What Teachers Say about Children in America." *Educational Leadership*, 46 (9), pp. 73–75.

Clark, R. (1983). *Family Life and School Achievement: Why Poor Black Children Succeed or Fail.* Chicago: University of Chicago Press.

Cutright, M. (1989). *The National PTA Talks to Parents: How to Get the Best Education for Your Child.* New York: Bantam Doubleday Dell.

Epstein, J. (1989). "On Parents and Schools: A Conversation with Joyce Epstein." *Educational Leadership*, 47 (2), pp. 24–27.

Henderson, A. (1981). *Parent Participation—Student Achievement: The Evidence Grows.* Columbia, Md.: National Committee for Citizens in Education.

Henderson, A. (1987). *The Evidence Continues to Grow: Parent Involvement Improves Student Achievement.* Columbia, Md.: National Committee for Citizens in Education.

Henderson, A. (1988). "Parents Are a School's Best Friend." *Phi Delta Kappan*, 70 (2), pp. 148–153.

Janus, M., et al. (1988). *Adolescent Runaways: Causes and Consequences.* Lexington, Mass.: Lexington Books.

Joan, P. (1986). *Preventing Teenage Suicide: The Living Alternative Handbook.* Edison, N.J.: Human Science Press.

Lindle, J. (1989). "What Do Parents Want from Principal and Teachers?" *Educational Leadership*, 37 (2), pp. 12–14.

McGuire, P. (1988). *Putting It Together: Teenagers Talk about Family Breakup.* New York: Delacorte Press.

Moles, O. (1982). "Synthesis of Research on Parent Participation in Children's Education." *Educational Leadership*, 39 (2), pp. 44–46.

Murphy, D. (1988). "The Just Community at Birch Meadows Elementary School." *Phi Delta Kappan*, 69 (6), pp. 427–428.

North Carolina Department of Public Instruction (1976). *Discipline in Schools: A Source Book.* Raleigh, N.C.: North Carolina Department of Education, p. 97.

Seeman, H. (1988). *Preventing Classroom Discipline Problems.* Lancaster, Pa.: Technomic Publishing Company.

Chapter
8

A Philosophy of Management and Discipline

A PHILOSOPHY

This book identifies and makes suggestions for using fundamental, generic principles of management and teaching discipline in elementary and secondary schools. The principles presented were derived from current research findings, well-known discipline models, and the individual and collective wisdom of a host of experienced teachers. The suggestions for implementing the selected principles of management and discipline represent a wide variety of approaches gathered from discipline models and teachers from around the United States and the Caribbean. Because no one methodology or approach works all the time with all students in all situations, the principles and implementation suggestions are an eclectic collection of ideas that reflect interventionist, noninterventionist and interactionalist philosophies.

In Chapter 1 noninterventionist teachers were characterized as those who believe students learn to behave appropriately because they are rational, reasonable human beings and who will, if given the opportunity, behave appropriately in their environment. These teachers use their authority and power sparingly and subtly to help students use their own inner reason.

Teacher interventionists were said to believe a student learns to behave appropriately as a result of his or her interactions with the outside environment. They believe the environment must be used to influence students to behave, and they freely use authority and power to secure desirable behavior. Interactionalist teachers were said to believe that both the students' inner reason and the outside environment interact to influence them to behave in appropriate ways (Wolfgang and Glickman, 1980).

The principles of discipline and management suggested in this book reflect all three of these interpretations of student behavior. Some of them imply students are molded and shaped by external forces; other imply internal motivations shape student behavior; and others suggest the importance of the interaction between internal reason and the external environment.

Although all three philosophical positions are reflected in this collection of behavior and management principles, the underlying belief is that most students will, if given the opportunity, behave appropriately. There is also the assumption that effective managers recognize those students and behavior problems which require teacher intervention and that they will react accordingly. For example, they know some students will willingly observe rules, others will require instruction and practice to learn to observe the rules, and still others may have to be coerced into observing the rules. The essential principles recognize that developmental levels of student behavior must be taken into account. Many of them support the noninterventionist and interactionalist philosophies; others allow for respectful intervention, if necessary.

SUMMARY OF ESSENTIAL PRINCIPLES

A brief summary of principles essential to effective management and teaching of discipline follows. Note that these principles collectively reflect more than simply maintaining law and order in classrooms; they also say that students want and can learn self-discipline; they send a message of caring and respect.

In Part One we found that in order for teachers to be able to establish a classroom climate where students can and will behave appropriately, teachers must have certain attitudes and attributes. They are as follows:

1. Effective managers respect students and have students' respect.

2. Effective managers are consistent, credible and dependable.
4. Effective managers value and enjoy learning themselves and expect students to do the same.
5. Effective managers communicate and model respect, consistency, credibility, dependability, valuing learning, and responsibility for learning; and they expect the same of students.

Part Two emphasized that effective managers plan to prevent discipline problems. Specifically, the principles state that:

6. Effective managers establish rules and procedures prior to or at the beginning of school.
7. Effective managers teach rules and procedures.
8. Effective managers know students and let students know them.
9. Effective managers care about students, and students know they care.
10. Effective managers exhibit with-it-ness.
11. Effective managers monitor to prevent behavior problems.

In Part Two we also found that effective managers prevent problems by maximizing student attention to and participation in the learning task.

12. Effective managers see to it that students utilize time allocated for learning.
13. Effective managers hold appropriate and realistic expectations for student achievement and behavior.
14. Effective managers provide interesting, meaningful seatwork and monitor for understanding.
15. Effective managers pace instruction to maximize student attention.
16. Effective managers give feedback that motivates and maximizes students' attention.
17. Effective managers encourage and secure students' active participation in learning.
18. Effective managers *plan* to resolve problems of inattention.

The importance of resolving problems of inappropriate behavior in appropriate ways is the focus of the following principles of management and teaching discipline found in Part Three:

19. Effective managers use desists to resolve inappropriate behavior.
20. Effective managers resolve problems by changing the learning environment.
21. Effective managers use the problem-solving approach to resolve misbehavior.
22. Effective managers use contracting to resolve behavior problems.
23. Effective managers use socialization as a way to resolve problem behavior.
24. Effective managers avoid harsh punishment.

The following principles indicate that effective managers teach self-discipline:

25. Effective managers model self-discipline.
26. Effective managers make it possible for students to practice appropriate behavior.
27. Effective managers seek alternatives to punishment.
28. Effective managers use feedback to teach self-discipline.
29. Effective managers avoid criticism.
30. Effective managers avoid student-teacher conflicts.
31. Effective managers use praise effectively.
32. Effective managers hold students accountable for behavior.
33. Effective managers use a grading system that students understand.

And listed last are two principles that assist with the implementation of all others.

34. Effective managers plan for the behavior of specific students in specific situations.
35. Effective managers involve parents in resolving behavior problems.

You should be aware by now that the appropriate use of many of these principles will require practice. For example, many teachers will need to practice effective praise and feedback deliberately. Other principles, such as holding students accountable and helping students understand their grades, can be implemented through planning and effort. Still other principles, such as modeling respect and avoiding criticism, will require changing our attitudes as well as our behavior.

You should remember that your success and that of students should be measured by the progress you make toward an effectively managed classroom where students learn self-discipline. You must also remember that the ultimate goal of using these principles is that both teachers and students will practice and learn self-discipline. Teachers who succeed in learning and teaching self-discipline achieve quality of purpose; they not only succeed but also achieve something beyond success—excellence.

QUESTIONS AND ACTIVITIES

8.1 Write an essay which completes the following: "If I were the best teacher in the world, I would. . . ." Be as specific as you can.

8.2 The importance of planning for behavior has been emphasized throughout this book. List some aspects of managing a classroom and teaching discipline for which you can plan.

8.3 What is your philosophy of discipline and child development?

8.4 Do you believe that all the principles of management and discipline are compatible with all philosophies of child development? Why? Why not?

8.5 Choose one of the principles and list as many suggestions for implementation as you can.

8.6 Which principles do you think are most important? Why?

8.7 Are there any "principles" that have not been included and that you would include as essential?

8.8 Throughout this book you have been asked to envision the kind of classroom you would like to lead. Describe that vision.

REFERENCES

Benninga, J. (1988). "An Emerging Synthesis in Moral Education." *Phi Delta Kappan, 69* (6) pp. 415–418.

Bloom, B. (1985). *Developing Talent in Young People*. New York: Ballantine Books.

Duke, D., and Meckel, A. (1984). *Teacher's Guide to Classroom Management*. New York: Random House.

Emmer, E., Evertson, C., Sanford, J., Clements, B., and Worsham, M. (1989). *Classroom Management for Secondary Teachers* (2nd ed.). Englewood Cliffs, N.J.: Prentice-Hall.

Etzion, A. (1982). "The Role of Self-Discipline." *Phi Delta Kappan, 64,* (3) pp. 184–187.

Evertson, C., Emmer, E., Clements, B., Sanford, J., and Worsham, M. (1989). *Classroom Management for Elementary Teachers* (2nd ed.). Englewood Cliffs, N.J.: Prentice-Hall.

Good, T., and Brophy, J. (1987). *Looking in Classrooms* (4th ed.). New York: Harper and Row.

Hall, R. V., and Hall, M. C. (1980). *How to use Systematic Attention and Approval (Social Reinforcement).* Austin, Tex.: Pro-ed.

Jersild, A. (1955). *When Teachers Face Themselves.* New York: Teachers College Press, Columbia University.

Lickona, T. (1988). "Four Strategies for Fostering Character Development in Children." *Phi Delta Kappan, 69* (6), pp. 419–423.

McDaniel, T. (1984). "Developing the Skills of Humanistic Discipline." *Educational Leadership, 41* (8), pp. 71–74.

McDaniel, T. (1989). "The Discipline Debate: A Road through the Thicket. *Educational Leadership, 46* (6), pp. 81–82.

Medland, M. and Vitale, M. (1984). *Management of Classrooms.* New York: Holt, Rinehart and Winston.

Sparzo, F., and Poteet, J. (1989). *Classroom Behavior: Detecting and Correcting Special Problems.* Boston: Allyn and Bacon.

Sprick, R. (1985). *Discipline in the Secondary Classroom.* West Nyack, N.J.: Center for Applied Research in Education, Inc.

Tracy, D. (1989). *The First Book of Common Sense Management.* New York: William Morris and Co.

Walker, J., and Shea, T. (1984). *Behavior Management: A Practical Approach for Educators* (3rd ed.). St. Louis: Time Mirror/Mosby College Publishing.

Weber, W., Crawford, J., Roff, L., and Robinson, C. (1983). *Classroom Management: Review of the Teacher Education and Research Literature.* Princeton, N.J.: Educational Testing Service.

Wolfgang, C., and Glickman, C. (1980). *Solving Discipline Problems.* Boston: Allyn and Bacon, pp. 246–247.

Index